Bombs Away

THE STORY OF A BOMBER TEAM

Bombs Away

THE STORY OF A BOMBER TEAM

Written for the U. S. Army Air Forces by

JOHN STEINBECK

With 60 Photographs by John Swope

PARAGON HOUSE · NEW YORK

FIRST PAPERBACK EDITION, 1990

PUBLISHED IN THE UNITED STATES BY

PARAGON HOUSE
90 FIFTH AVENUE
NEW YORK, NY 10011

REPRINTED BY ARRANGEMENT WITH VIKING PENGUIN, A DIVISON OF
PENGUIN BOOKS USA INC.

10   9   8   7   6   5   4   3   2

LIBRARY OF CONGRESS CATALOGING-IN-PUBLICATION DATA
STEINBECK, JOHN, 1902-1968.
BOMBS AWAY : THE STORY OF A BOMBER TEAM / WRITTEN FOR THE
U.S. ARMY AIR FORCES BY JOHN STEINBECK ; WITH 60 PHOTOGRAPHS
BY JOHN SWOPE.
P.   CM.
REPRINT. ORIGINALLY PUBLISHED: NEW YORK : VIKING PRESS, 1942.
ISBN 1-55778-311-X : $9.95
1. BOMBING, AERIAL—UNITED STATES.   2. UNITED STATES. ARMY AIR
FORCES.   3. FLIGHT CREWS—UNITED STATES.   I. TITLE.
UG703.S74   1990
358.4'2'0973—dc20   90-30555
CIP

THIS BOOK IS PRINTED ON ACID-FREE PAPER.
MANUFACTURED IN THE UNITED STATES OF AMERICA

PREFACE

A BOOK should have a dedication, I suppose, but this book is a dedication. It is a dedication to the men who have gone through the hard and rigid training of members of a bomber crew and who have gone away to defend the nation. This book is dedicated to those men, although it is not intended for their reading, for it would be primer work to them. This book is intended for the men of the future bomber teams and for their parents, for the people at home. Nowhere in this book is it indicated that it is easy to be a member of the crew. It is very difficult. But it may be an advantage to the prospective cadet or gunner, to the radio man or crew chief, to know what is in store for him when he makes application for the Air Force; and this book is intended to be read by the mothers and fathers of the prospective Air Force men, to the end that they will have some idea of the training their sons have undertaken. Their sons will not have time to tell about it once the training starts.

And mostly this book intends to tell the whole people of the kind and quality of our Air Force, of the caliber of its men and of the excellence of its equipment. There is one great difficulty in writing such a book as this. So rapid is the growth of the Air Force and so free is it from the strictures of tradition that changes are made every day. Thus by the time the book is finished and printed some of it is bound to be obsolete. That cannot be helped. The world is changing just as rapidly. One thing only does not change. The young men of now are the equals of any young men of our history. The scouts and fighters of our past have their counterparts in the present. The Air Force proves it. The Air Force proves the stupidity of the bewildered Europeans, who seeing this nation at peace, imagined that it was degenerate, who seeing that we fought and quarreled in our politics, took this indication of our energy as a sign of our decadence. The fortresses and the B-24's, the Airacobras, and the P-47's have by now disillusioned them.

The author wishes to thank the officers and men who helped him and taught him. They will not be thanked by name because that would be breaking an Air Force tradition. Lastly the title "Bombs Away" is taken from the call of the bombardier when the great bombs fall free of the racks and curve down toward the enemy. The bombardier in the transparent nose of the ship lifts his microphone and his voice goes into the ears of every member of the crew and he calls "Bombs Away." That means that the mission is completed, that means it is time to go home. Someday the call will ring above a broken enemy and then it will be time to go home for good.

A flight of At–9s

CONTENTS

ILLUSTRATIONS

INTRODUCTION

I N ALL HISTORY, probably no nation has tried more passionately or more thoughtfully to avoid fighting than the United States had tried to avoid the present war against Japan and Germany. During the years 1930 to 1940, the nation was preoccupied with internal difficulties, with problems of distribution and production not impossible of solution, but requiring thought and trial and error and some conflict. It is not possible to know whether a solution could have been reached nor how soon it could have been reached. But during that period when a direction had not been set, nor an end established, a generation of young men and young women were kept marking time, not knowing where they were going. In fact, concerned only with keeping alive until some direction was established toward which they could go. Young men coming out of the schools, finding no jobs, no goals, became first despondent and then cynical; a curious and muscling state of mind which was considered intellectual despair, but which was actually the product of mental and physical idleness, descended upon the youth of the country.

The young people were not unlike those clots of boys who hang around the fronts of poolrooms waiting for something to happen. An anarchy of thought and action had in fact settled over the young people of the country. An antidote for the poisons of this idleness and indirection might eventually have been found, some great building program for the betterment of the country (some economic direction or trend to tear away the lethargy). But meanwhile, with one set of certainties gone and no new set established, the country floundered about. Floundered about in fact so convincingly that our enemies considered us to be in a dying condition. Because we were uncertain, we tried to avoid the thought of war and the means of war and the preparation for war. Some of our leaders wished to cut the world in half—to defend this hemisphere against the other—while others thought it would be good business and good thinking to give England the weapon to fight the war for us.

Perhaps the future will show that we were very fortunate in that we were not being permitted to use either of these methods for the war. Our arguments and disunity might have kept us ineffective or only partly effective until it was too late. But Germany and Japan were bound to blunder sooner or later, and blunder they did. In attacking us they destroyed their greatest ally, our sluggishness, our selfishness, and our disunity.

The attack on us set in motion the most powerful species drive we know—that of survival. It created direction toward which we could aim all of our vitalities—and we have great vitality. What the Axis could not understand was that the measure of our unrest was the measure of our vitality. The war was dumped into our laps; we could not avoid it, but fortunately for us, we have been given a kind of war we are peculiarly capable of fighting—a war without established technique or method, a kind of war rooted in production in which we surpass. If we ourselves had chosen the kind of war to be fought, we could not have found one more suitable to our national genius. For this is a war of transport, of machines, of mass production, of flexibility, and of inventiveness, and in each of these fields we have been pioneers if not actual inventors.

With the very techniques required for this war, our people explored a continent and peopled it and developed it, threw rails across it, drove highways north and south, burrowed for metals, and dammed rivers for power. And the energy and versatility and initiative which developed this continent have not

14

died. Perhaps some of our difficulty before the beginning of this war was caused by the aliveness and the versatility and initiative without the goal.

Even the tactics now used in Europe and in China are not new to us; guerrilla fighting, commando fighting, our fathers learned from the Indians 200 years ago and practiced for 200 years.

Even the children playing in the vacant lots in America practice the tactics of the guerrilla and the commandos in their games, while speed, mechanics, and motors are almost born with them. In short, this is the kind of war that Americans are probably more capable of fighting and fighting better than any other people in the world.

The goal has been set now and we have an aim and a direction, and a kind of fierce joy runs through the country. The President set an end in production that was almost beyond reason and that end is being reached. The General Staff designed an army like none in the world and that army is being assembled and trained.

Ever since the end of the last war our more intelligent generals have foreseen what power would lie in the hands of the nation with a great and well-trained Air Force. These leaders have advocated the building of a huge Air Force and the training of thousands of pilots. But as always, opposition to change arose against them. They were denied facilities and money and, in one case at least, actual persecution was used.

It was only when Germany demonstrated so violently in Belgium, in Holland, in Norway, in Crete, how devastating air power could be, that this nation awakened to the fact that we must have a great Air Force. And we find now, that what Germany accomplished in eight years, we must surpass in less than two. In many ways this challenge is good for us. We are building the greatest Air Force in the world and we are training, developing, and grouping the most highly selected body of young men in the country to operate it.

The Air Force Training Commands are not making the mistake of trying to create a great Air Force with inferior products. Indeed, the physical and mental testing of applicants is so rigid that acceptance by the Air Force of a young man is proof that he is far above the normal in intelligence, in health, and in strength.

The planes are rolling off the assembly line by the thousand now and the men to fly them are being trained by the thousand. Hundreds of new airfields are being marked out all over the country. Into the induction centers every day, come truckloads of young men to begin their training and testing. And because the training has been so rapid and so without precedent, because the Air Force is making its tradition as it goes, a number of myths and stories and misconceptions have gotten loosed in the country.

A good example of this kind of myth is the often-repeated statement that the life of an air gunner is twenty minutes. How such a figure could have been arrived at and on what basis and by what comparison is impossible to find out. One might as accurately say that the life of a pedestrian is fifteen minutes or that the life of a man crossing a street is a half hour. It is amazing how these irresponsible statements persist. If a pedestrian gets hit by a car or a gunner gets hit by a bullet his life is over, and if he doesn't, he is still alive.

The development of our Air Force has been so rapid and the men who have designed it have been so busy that so far there has not been time to issue in a book the process whereby a young American boy becomes a pilot, a bombardier, a navigator, or a gunner. Young men may be a trifle apprehensive entering on a training the process and technique of which they do not understand. It is the intention of this book to set down in simple terms the nature and mission of a bomber crew and the technique and training of each member of it. For the bomber crew will have a great part in defending this country and in attacking its enemies. It is the greatest team in the world.

"A single-stack steamer was sighted . . ."

THE BOMBER

OF ALL branches of the Service, the Air Force must act with the least precedent, the least tradition. Nearly all tactics and formations of infantry have been tested over ten thousand years. Even tanks, although they operate at a high rate of speed, make use of tactics which were developed first by chariot and then by cavalry.

But the Air Force has no centuries of trial and error to study; it must feel its way, making its errors and correcting them. The whole technique of aerial fighting has a history of less than twenty years. While to some extent this lack of experience is limiting, in another sense, it allows the Air Force a freedom of action not quite possible in other branches of the Service; for armies, like other organizations, have a tendency to rely on tradition and to hold to traditional techniques after their efficacy has passed. The Air Force must make its way in a new field where there are no precedents, where there are few rules to fall back on. During the last war, military airplanes were used largely for observation. The heroic dog fights which took place over the lines in Europe were usually the result of one plane trying to keep another from seeing what was going on behind the line.

It was only toward the very end of the war that bombers began to be built and bombing tactics developed. During the period between the two wars, most of the nations of the world experimented expensively with airplanes. The world at large was so tired of war, so sick with war that it hoped it might never have to use these experiments. Of all the nations of the world, only Germany knew what it was going to do and where it was

19

going with its aircraft. Germany, and the dark Aryans of Italy and the yellow Aryans of Japan developed air forces. The purpose was to blast and maim and kill. They knew exactly what they were going to do. They developed plane types for specific purposes and they watched the rest of the world for the uncorrelated experiments which they might devote to their purposes. Thus when the United States Navy developed the principle of dive-bombing, Germany took the principle and welded it into its air tactics and later used it overwhelmingly on the nations it attacked.

Japan studied the intricacies of the American supercharger and incorporated it in its Zero fighter. The Axis developed and took and bought and stole the unrelated air inventions of the whole world and gathered them together into a destructive design, and when the Axis struck at Europe with this carefully designed unit of destruction it found Europe unprepared to meet it. The Axis had been practicing with its new weapon in Ethiopia, in Spain, and in China, and the rest of the world took little notice. Wild Ethiopian horsemen had been bombed and machine gunned on the ground to teach young Mussolinis how to use their weapons. The people of Guernica were cut down, Madrid was bombed, Barcelona destroyed, to train the Axis how to use its weapons. China defended itself with a wall of men against a wall of metal. And only after Europe was attacked and half beaten did the people of the world awake to the fact that air power can only be beaten with air power. If the German plan had worked we would have been lost, for the Axis planned to destroy us before our factories could begin turning out planes, before our young men could be trained to operate them. Holland, Belgium, and France were gone—surprised and blasted before they could resist—and then the German bombers struck at England; for the intention was to destroy England as quickly and as completely as France had been destroyed, to

20

wreck the small English Air Force on the ground and to destroy the cities and bring the people to their knees.

But from England a few Spitfires went up to meet the German bombers which for the first time were challenged. And probably the history of the world for all time to come was changed by those few Spitfires and the young men who flew them. For the first time the Axis had air power against it no matter how inade-quate. Those few Spitfires gave us time and gave England time to build the weapon to destroy the Axis—the weapon of air power, faster, bigger, and more numerous than the Axis can provide. At last the world is awake. It knows now that it could not escape the war and that the only way to terminate the war is to destroy the men and the weapons that caused it.

The weapons of the Air Force and their use are changing and developing very rapidly, but already certain facts that were known to a few of the leaders of our Air Force are becoming generally known. We know now that the champion, that the backbone of air power is the heavy bomber. Pursuit plane, torpedo plane, observation plane have specialized services very necessary and very vital as part of the Air Force, but the puncher is the heavy bomber.

For a long time we hated the idea of the heavy bomber. It was considered only an offensive weapon designed to carry bomb loads to enemy cities to destroy them. But very recently a new factor has emerged. The Coral Sea and the Battle of Midway have demonstrated that our heavy bomber is our greatest weapon for the defense of our coast against invasion.

In the short time of its use the heavy bomber has made a tremendous record. It may, in fact, have changed the nature of warfare in the world. In the Coral Sea long-range heavy bombers, land-based, went out to meet the Japanese invasion fleet and broke its back, dispersed its ships. And again at Midway, the long-range bombers found a Japanese fleet and dis-

21

persed it before it could near land. These terrible weapons may have changed the nature of navies, may have made capital ships obsolete. From offensive weapons, the long-range bombers have taken their place as our greatest defensive weapon, and we know now that our coast cannot be attacked by invasion fleets as long as we have great numbers of long-range bombers to find the enemy at sea and destroy him before he can make contact with our shores.

The enormous cruising range of our bombers, together with their capacity for carrying enormous quantities and weights of bombs, have put new emphasis, new responsibility, and new honor on the land-based, long-range bomber. It can patrol and strike thousands of miles at sea and no ship, no matter how protected, can survive the weight of its attack. On the newly formed and trained bomber crews is being placed the first responsibility to the nation, to defend the coasts and to carry the war to the enemy. There can be little question why the Army Air Force is placing such emphasis on the heavy bomber.

In the earlier days of the Service, young men entering the Air Force wished first to be pilots and second to be pilots of pursuit ships. The speed of the ships and the dramatic gallantry of the action drew the best of our young men to that Service. But the pursuit ship is a short-range, supplementary weapon compared to the bomber. In the Air Force, a new, compact, and exciting organization is growing up—the bomber crew. It's really a bomber team and it can truly be called a team for it must have those qualities which make a good football team, a good basketball team. It must function as a unit. It must have complete discipline and yet it must delegate its responsibilities. Each member of a bomber crew has a function to perform which must come out of himself. Each member of a bomber crew has two functions—that of command as well as that of obedience.

22

The pilot and the copilot must fly the ship, that is true, but they must take their directions from the navigator, for he knows where they are and where they are going and how to get there. Arriving at the target, the bombardier must take command, for it is he who must drop the bombs on their target, who must destroy the ship or break up the power line or riddle the factory. And all during flight, the engineer commands the engines and sees that they function. The radio man is the voice and ears of the plane, keeping it in contact with its squadron and with its base, and all the time the aerial gunners are charged with the defense of the ship. On the sharpness of their eyes and the accuracy of their aim the safety of the whole crew depends.

This is truly a team, each member responsible to the whole and the whole responsible to the members. And only with its teamlike quality can the bomber successfully function. Here is no commander with subordinates, but a group of responsible individuals functioning as a unit while each member exercises individual judgment and foresight and care.

This is the kind of an organization that Americans above all others are best capable of maintaining. The bomber team is truly a democratic organization. No single man can give all the orders to make a bomber effective. The effectiveness of its mission rests on the initiative and judgment of each one of its members. Not everyone on a football team insists on being quarterback. He plays the position he is best fitted to play. The best football team is one where every member plays his own particular game as a part of the team. The best bomber team is the one where each man plays for the success of the mission.

Thus, because of the foresight of the leaders of our Air Force, a change is coming over the attitude of the young men who are joining. There was a time when a navigator was a pilot who had failed and had taken second choice, when a bombardier was a navigator who had failed and had taken sec-

Boeing B—17 E, commonly known as the Flying Fortress

ond choice. That is no longer true. A pilot is one kind of man, having one kind of qualities. He might not make a good navigator. A navigator might not make a good pilot nor a good bombardier, while a bombardier requires certain physical and mental traits which are different from those required by either navigator or pilot.

So that each man will do the work he is best fitted to do, the Air Force has devised a series of tests, mental, manual, and physical, which strongly indicate the position in the bomber each applicant should take.

America is building two kinds of long-range bombers for its rapidly developing bomber crews, while other kinds of ships are being built and tested. It is probable that the B-17, popularly known as the Flying Fortress, and the B-24, which the

Consolidated B–24, commonly known as the Liberator

British call the Liberator and for which we have no name yet, will be the nucleus and the backbone of the Air Force striking power. Both are four-engined ships capable of great cruising range and of large bomb-carrying capacity, and although they do not look alike at all they seem to be about equal in effectiveness. But such are the loyalties of Americans toward their tools and their weapons that a Flying Fortress crew will spend a night arguing for the Flying Fortress, while a B-24 crew defends its ship with some heat. The B-17, or Flying Fortress, is the best known and better publicized of the two ships. Its name has struck a responsive chord in the public mind, in spite of the fact that its name does not describe it at all. It is in no sense a fortress, it is an attack ship. Its purpose is to carry the war to an enemy, not to sit still and repel attack. Such has been the

25

appeal of its name that all large bombers are known in the press and in the public mind as Flying Fortresses.

The B-17 has long wings and a graceful and serene flight. It is so large that it does not seem to fly very fast. It is a graceful and beautiful ship, capable of great altitude.

The B-24, on the other hand, is an earnest, deadly-looking ship—pugnacious, stubby. Its wings having a different air foil from that of the B-17 seem short and stubby by comparison. On the ground, sitting on its tricycle landing gear, its tail in the air, it looks like an *Anopheles* mosquito. Looked at from the side, it seems thick and clumsy, but head on it is lean and streamlined. Its bomb bays slide up its side like the top of a rolled-top desk and it takes the air with a roar of menace. The crews of the B-24 defend it valiantly against the aspersion that the B-17 is better.

Actually, these two ships seem to be about equal in performance, although they are so different in appearance. The tradition originated by truck drivers is carried out in these ships. They are given names by their crews and the names painted on the sides, Little Eva, Elsie, Alice, are in line with the American trait of establishing a kind of affectionate relationship with his machine, of endowing it with life and with personality. And airplanes do have, in common with boats, certain personal traits —no two fly quite alike, each one has its little quirks and crankinesses, its excellencies and failings.

Both B-17 and B-24 bristle with defensive machine guns, in the nose, in top, in belly turrets, and in the tail so that every inch of it is covered against attack. American assembly lines are turning out these two planes in great numbers for the Army Air Forces. The huge bomber production plants swarm with men and women working 24 hours a day in shifts which keep the assembly line moving all the time. In the parts plants, wings, tails, parts of fuselage are welded and riveted. Engine plants build and test the motive power, instruments and electrical wiring are assembled and made ready; the noise of lathes and stamps and little riveting machines is deafening, and all these parts move toward the assembly line. And then to the first station come fuselage and center wing structure and all are braced together, fitted and riveted and made strong, and the assembly moves on a track to the next station. At each station are crews trained to do specific things and as the line moves from station to station, the plane takes shape; engines and supercharges are installed, wiring and wing tips and flaps, de-icers and turrets and guns, from station to station, growing and inspected— radios, propellers, and armor plates, landing gear and wheels and giant tires. The ship grows from parts and pieces, built by station crews who know their work so well that they do not even seem to hurry. The great planes move down the line until they reach the end and roll away—finished.

The wing section of a B—24 being lifted into place

At each station they have been inspected rigorously and when at last they are pulled to the flight line, they are given a final inspection. The engines are started, tested, and proved, and every working part is checked, and finally the test pilots take their places. A new ship roars down the runway and takes to the air, to be given as violent a testing as it is possible to devise. Then it is brought to the ground and checked again and only then is it accepted by the Army Air Forces. These are the ships of the line, these are the champions, these are the weapons and tools of the bomber crew. They are as good as or better than anything like them in the world.

What ingenuity can contrive in metal and instrument has been contrived. While the ships were being built, bomber crews were being trained all over the country to be assembled at last for their missions. The long-range bomber is an intricate and marvelous machine capable of climbing to great altitude, capable of tremendous range, capable of carrying great bomb loads; but it is still only as good as its bomber crew. It is only a machine. It can only fly as well as its pilot can fly it and only arrive at the point toward which its navigator can direct it.

Marvelous and accurate as the American bombsight is, it still must rely upon the steadiness and judgment of the bombardier, while the sleek sides of the bomber and the lives of the bomber crew are dependent upon the marksmanship and the coolness and the judgment of the aerial gunners. We know that our long-range bombers are as good as, or better than, any like planes in the world; and we believe that in the raw material of the young men of the United States we have potential bomber crews which are better than anything in the world. This is not vain hope nor wishful thinking, but is rooted in the background and home training of the young men who will make up the bomber crews of the future. The boys, who in school are making intricate little models of balsa wood, are the flyers of the future.

Even now, the recognition models being used by the Army for the training of observers are being built in the high schools. But beyond the making of models and the association with airplanes, our young men have in their backgrounds associations and trainings which make them ideal crews for bombers. For example, a fine horseman usually makes a fine pilot. The association between man and animal is very like that of association between pilot and machine. The ideal pilot does not push his machine about, but urges it, becomes almost a part of it, and the analogy is even closer than that. In basic training planes, the co-ordination between feet and hands on stick and rudder is very like the same co-ordination of pressure on stirrup and reins of a horseman. Beyond this, our boys and young men of the towns and farms have machinery in their souls. Two generations of young men have couped up their cut-down Fords, have kept them going with spit and wire long after they should have gone on the junk heap, have torn them down and rebuilt them, until they know every polished surface, every scarred and worn bearing, every pitted cylinder. Keeping their crazy cars going, they have learned motors more completely than they could have in any other way. Experimenting to get every last ounce of speed out of their aging motors, tinkering their carburetors to get every last possible mile out of their gasoline, these boys in high schools and on the farms know motors as few people in the world know them; and Army instructors say that these young men make the best possible flyers—the farm boys who have kept the old tractors pounding over the land after they were worn out.

And we may be thankful that frightened civil authorities and specific Ladies Clubs have not managed to eradicate from the country the tradition of the possession and use of firearms, that profound and almost instinctive tradition of Americans. For one does not really learn to shoot a rifle or a machine gun in a few weeks. Army gunnery instructors have thus described a perfect machine gunner: When he was six years old, his father gave him a .22 rifle and taught him to respect it as a dangerous weapon, and taught him to shoot it at a target. At nine, the boy ranged the hills and the woods, hunting squirrels, until the pointing of his rifle was as natural to him as the pointing of his finger. At twelve, the boy was given his first shotgun and taken duck hunting, quail hunting, and grouse hunting; and where, with the rifle, he had learned accuracy in pointing, he now learned the principle of leading a moving target, learned instinctively that you do not fire *at* the moving target, but ahead of it, and learned particularly that his gun is a deadly weapon, always to be respected and cared for. When such a boy enters the Air Force, he has the whole background of aerial gunnery in him before he starts, and he has only to learn the mechanism of a new weapon, for the principles of shooting down enemy airplanes are exactly those of shooting duck. Such a boy, with such a background, makes the ideal aerial gunner, and there are hundreds of thousands of them in America. Luckily for us, our tradition of bearing arms has not gone from the country, and the tradition is so deep and so dear to us that it is one of the most treasured parts of the Bill of Rights—the right of all Americans to bear arms, with the implication that they will know how to use them.

Thus we see that we have in America individual young men who will make great members of bomber crews, but we have another tradition and another practice which guarantees that these crews will be able to act as units. From the time of their being able to walk, our boys and girls take part in team playing. From one ol' cat to basketball, to sand-lot baseball, to football, American boys learn instinctively to react as members of a team. They learn that not everyone can be pitcher or quarterback, but that each team must be a balance of various skills. And in this

30

Mid-section of a B—24 on the assembly line

instinct for team play and team reaction the Air Force finds its material for the greatest team of this emergency—the bomber crew; for the bomber crews are the close-knit teams which will defend our goal posts and drive deep into the territory of the enemy. And it is the training of the individual members of the bomber crew and its final assembling into a close-knit team that this book will discuss.

The Army Air Force is recruiting thousands of young men, and they must be a very special kind of young men. They must, in fact, be the best physical and mental specimens the country produces. A young man making application for the Army Air Force should have very definite qualities. In the first place, he should have parents who are so proud of him and so proud of the country that they will help him to enter the Service and encourage him in entering it. And, if he should be accepted by the Air Force, his parents will have every reason to be proud of him; for his mother to wear the insignia of the Air Forces is to prove beyond any doubt that she has produced a son far above the average in intelligence and physique. It is better if the boy has gone two years to college, but it is not essential. Graduation from high school is sufficient. He should not enter the Service with any martyrish complex about dying for his country. Such German and Japanese inculcations make soldiers good only to a certain point, but they are far from the American tradition. The best soldier in the world is not one who anticipates death with pleasure or with the ecstatic anticipation of Valhalla, honor, and glory, but the one who fights to win and to survive. There is no place in the Air Force for pseudo-religious martyrdom. Further, the young man should enter the Air Force knowing that his service need not end with the end of the war, that he is undertaking, if he wishes, a career for his whole life; for there is little doubt that, at the end of this war, the development of this nation, and of the hemisphere, and of the world, will be very closely tied to the use of the airplane.

If the young man in school has been interested in physics and in mathematics and in general science, it will be easier for him. It would be well if he has driven a car or a boat and has tinkered with motors. While these things are not absolutely necessary, the young man who has them will find that he is two steps ahead of the rest. The applicant should be capable of individual judgment, for the Air Force is not an organization of commander and dull followers. It cannot be. Every member of the Air Force, from ground crew mechanic to squadron commander, must make thousands of personal and individual decisions constantly. The Air Force is much more a collaboration than a command.

It is well if the applicant has played on various teams in his school—basketball, football, water polo, baseball—for in team play the lessons of responsible co-operation are best and most deeply learned. Physically the applicant need not be large. In fact, in some cases it is better if he is small. But he must be very healthy, and he must have no physical disability of any kind. He cannot have defective eyesight or color blindness. But beyond simple physical fitness, he must have other qualities. His manual co-ordination must be above the average. The discipline of limb and muscle must be perfect, and, while he need not be finely trained, he must have a physical system which will respond to the rigid training of the Air Force to emerge a toughened, disciplined soldier.

Beyond these things, the young man should have great faith in his country, in its future and its future greatness, and he should have a sense of his relation to that future and of his responsibility toward his country's future, for he will emerge from the war in a position of leadership and in the postwar peaceful world he will have a strong hand.

A young man having these qualities should make application to join the United States Army Air Force. He should not specify

33

that he wants to be a pilot or a navigator or a bombardier or a gunner, a radio operator or an engineer. The Air Force will give him tests which will prove definitely which position he is most capable of filling, for a man who is capable of being a good pilot need not at all be a good navigator, while a good navigator need not be a good bombardier. Each one has special qualities, and careful Army psychological and physical tests will prove which qualities the applicant has. Lastly, the young man wishing to enter the Air Force should not for a moment get the idea that he is going into something easy. There is neither time nor room for softness or laziness in the Air Force. The cadet will work harder and longer than he thought he could. He will study harder than he has ever studied in school. He will play violently and eat enormously and he will emerge tough, competent, and sure. He will be a crew mate in the hardest-hitting, most competent team this country has ever produced. This is really the Big League in the toughest game we have ever been up against, with the pennant the survival and future of the whole nation.

If the training of a bomber crew is hard, it is hard for a purpose. For great responsibilities are put into the hands of these young men: the simple responsibility for the expensive and intricate machine that is the bombing plane, responsibility for the secrecy of the bomb sight, and beyond these the greatest responsibility of all, for to a large extent the bomber team will be responsible for the safety and survival of the nation.

The Army Air Force has been given an incredible job to do. Few people on the outside realize the magnitude of its mission. It has been simply ordered to produce the greatest air force in the world and it must do much more than to build fields, train pilots, develop tactics and formations. It must, for example, build thousands of airfields all over the country, training fields and auxiliary fields and emergency landing fields, and these are being leveled, built, and commissioned at an incredible rate of speed. It must establish schools for the various specialists and train instructors to train personnel. The Air Force is different from other military organizations. It must delegate its authority to the ground crew mechanic who is as responsible for the flight of a plane as the pilot. On the airfields barracks are going up. They are hardly completed before they are filled. On some fields the cadets live in tents until their barracks are finished.

The Air Force must inspect and supervise the assembly lines that are turning out the planes, test them and accept them for the service. It must clear the way for metals and supplies, engines and instruments. There can be no inferior part in an air force. The problems of supply alone are incalculable—supplies of food and uniforms and games, supplies of bombs and practice bombs—and at the same time that it is a training Air Force, it must also be a fighting Air Force. Our bombers and pursuit planes are in action in Australia, in the Orient, in Europe, and in Africa. Every day the papers have accounts of Air Force action in some part of the world, and every day, truckloads of boys who have applied for entrance to the Air Force are picked up at the station and brought to the induction centers to enter the hard and satisfying training of the Air Force. They are disheveled and tired when they arrive at the induction centers and they are dressed in all manner of clothes, some in overalls, some in sweaters and slacks, and some more fortunate arrive in their own cars and they have suitcases, bundles, and brief cases and those last gifts which doting parents bestow on their sons. Some of them are a little uneasy and a little homesick and nearly all of them are slightly apprehensive because they do not know what is going to happen to them next. It is part of the purpose of this book to tell them in advance what is going to happen to them next, to tell them the process by which they will become members of the Air

Force. So far there has been no way for them to find out before induction. Every move has its purpose but until now there has not been time to tell the inductees in advance the purpose of each move.

Suppose a young farmer from South Carolina and a young graduate of a small college looking for a job and an Idaho trumpet player all have made applications for the Air Force, have been accepted for induction, have been given their orders and their transportation, so that they end up at last with two hundred and fifty others at a railroad station near an induction center. They have ridden a long time and they are tired, dusty, and dispirited. The two hundred and fifty are a long way from home, they haven't had time to make friends. Their speech has affectual accents of Maine, of the Middle West, of the South, and the Southwest, and each one thinks the rest sound rather funny and each one is a little bit afraid of all the rest and feels that he is among strangers. They get down at the station, carrying their miscellaneous baggage. There they are met by an officer who checks their names against his list, lines them up, and assigns them to trucks, and loaded in the Army trucks they are taken to the induction center.

At the induction center, the cadet master takes them in hand and from now on they will have little time to be lonely or dispirited. Quickly they are lined up and assigned to quarters and then they are marched to the barber shop where they suffer what to a civilian is an indignity—their hair is cut short. These haircuts soon come to be affectionately known by the names of their fields, such as the Randolph Roach or the Kelly Clip. If it is summer, they have abandoned their civilian coats by now and their shirts, and some of them have abandoned their undershirts and they march now to a most searching physical examination.

The medical specialists are arranged by sections. Eyes are rigidly tested not only for weakness, but for color blindness.

36

Ears are examined. Chests are X-rayed for any pulmonary weakness. Bones and feet are examined for any deformity. Blood tests are taken to determine any venereal disease. They sit a time with the psychiatrist who questions them closely to see whether they might not have some fixation which would unfit them for the Service, some fear of heights or closed places, some psychic abnormality. They are questioned about past illnesses, diseases, which might have left a degenerative scar. Quick though it is, few men have ever been more closely inspected, and when it is complete their medical history is compiled and their health background established. If something is wrong with an applicant which can be treated, treatment is prescribed and begun. And when the examinations are complete the inoculations begin, serums for typhoid, yellow fever, for tetanus, small pox—all the preventives known that will save them from future illness.

The medical examination has now been completed. Some of the candidates will go back to the medical center for treatment of minor ailments or dentistry, but their first inspection is done. Now they go to a long office room where each one is interviewed, his insurance papers are made out, and he is given a number by which he will be known during the whole time he is in the Army. Under this number his pay will be issued and under this number his medical and his military career will be filed away. He will wear his number on a tag hung around his neck and he must know his number as well as his name, for in the Army there may be duplications of names but there are no duplications of numbers; and if this seems a little cold and prisonlike, at least it is more efficient than the simple use of names. His number is his exact identification.

From the office, the candidates go to the quartermaster, where they are issued their uniforms, their work clothes, and their athletic clothes; khaki shirts and trousers for the summer, with

Preliminary examination at an Induction Center

overseas caps and ornaments which are distinctive in the whole Army; for work clothes gray coveralls are issued—one-piece garments which cover the whole body. These are standard garments for the flying line and for flying. And since the cadets must be hardened quickly, athletic clothes are issued—shorts and uppers and tennis shoes. For during every moment of spare time during the day, the cadets will be active, playing baseball, volleyball and basketball. There is no time to sit about during cadet training.

The physical testing of the candidate is now over but the mental testing is about to begin. The Air Force must have men above the average in mentality and in co-ordination. By now all

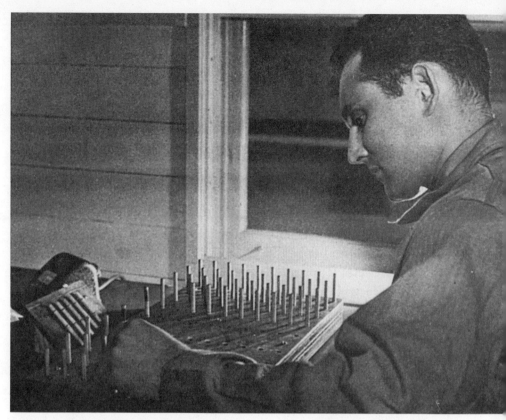

Coordination test of placing pegs of various lengths into their right holes

movements about the post are executed in formation. The candidates march to the long narrow room in which the intelligence tests will be given. Each man has a desk which is a little stall, whose sides and front are raised above eye level. A man may look over his barrier at the instructor at the front of the room but he cannot see sideways at the other men being tested. This semiprivacy has a tendency to make the man being tested less nervous. First the instructor explains the tests and how they are to be taken. Forms and questions are printed on the examination paper. The answers are given by checking one of a number of possible boxes. There is enough metal in the pencils to make an electrical contact, so that when the tests are finished they are put

39

in a machine and graded automatically and mechanically. This not only makes it impossible for any favoritism to be shown, but also is much quicker and more accurate.

Each section of these intelligence tests has been set down to determine some separate quality of the mind. Thus forms nearly alike are checked to determine judgment of eye and mind, meter readings on blind gauges are used to test the sense of interval, parallel and nonparallel sentences and figures are included to test the judgment and imagination. The tests do not determine the amount of education the candidate has but the quality of his awareness. If his mind is alert, he will have noticed things all his life which have not been noticed by a duller mind; and if his mind is alert, he will notice things in these tests that a duller mind would not perceive. The intelligence test is really an awareness test showing whether the eyes see and the ears hear and the brain correlates what is going on about a man, and since a member of the Air Force in the course of his duty must be extremely aware, these tests indicate the threshold of his awareness.

The aware brain which suffers from sensitiveness, from self-consciousness, from nervousness, need not be afraid of these tests, for such factors are taken into consideration. No likely candidate is thrown out because he happens to be nervous or worried. These basic intelligence tests establish whether the candidate is a fit prospect for the Air Force; but when he has passed his basic tests, there are others designed to show what branch of the Service he will do best in.

The manual and mental aptitude tests are extremely interesting and they are not taken once but a number of times; for a first good score is not nearly so important as the improvement shown in a second over a first and in a third over a second. These tests are designed to show the speed with which a man can learn mental and physical techniques, and it sometimes happens that a candidate who makes a first good score does not improve. The bad beginner who learns rapidly is much more desirable in the Air Force.

These tests are of many kinds, from the simple manual co-ordination test which consists of rapidly turning pegs over in holes, the manual concentration test of plunging a stylus into holes set in a rapidly revolving cylinder, the maintaining of contact through a wire with a small metal plate set eccentrically on a revolving disc, to a rather complicated two-hand co-ordination test where each hand must act independently to achieve a desired end. But always it is not the first cleverness of the candidate which counts, but his ability to improve. From all these tests a fairly clear picture is arrived at concerning the mentality, the co-ordination, the judgment and speed of making decisions, the versatility and reaction time of each individual applicant for the Air Force.

The Air Force has drawn on the best psychologists in the nation in devising these tests. Many men who recently were conducting researches in our universities are now commissioned in the Service to devise and to supervise the testing of young men. Never before in our Army have such rigid examinations been used, and if a great deal of time and effort are given to this phase of induction there is a very good reason for it. A young man, otherwise perfect, may have some block in his nervous response system which is not at all apparent. If such a condition were not discovered by tests, he would go on to his instructors. He might indeed be well along in his training before some emergency showed up his trouble. In such a case a great deal of valuable time would have been wasted on him. He could perhaps even go so far that his difficulty might endanger the ship and the crew or a mission. The rigid tests are set up to find such difficulties in the candidates before they have used up the training time of instructors. And so for several days the candidates

"Baseball teams sprout from the fields . . ."

go into little rooms where the testing devices are. There they sit or stand with only a technical sergeant present and there the secrets of their nervous responses are unfailingly brought out and recorded. After the war the wealth of material from these thousands of tests will be invaluable to research in psychology by the men who search for causes of various nervous reactions. But now, when the tests are completed, the candidate who has passed will not be likely through some unknown quirk to fall down on the job given him to do.

During these days of induction much has happened to the candidates besides their examinations. They have begun to learn military formations, the basic evolutions of soldiers, the manual of arms which all soldiers must know; and although they may be very tired at night, so tired that they fall into their cots and sleep profoundly, a change has begun to be apparent in them. Their bodies are straightening, their heads are held a little higher, a spring has come into their steps. This change has taken place so rapidly that it is astonishing. The bad posture, the sloppy bearing of the riders in the truck to the induction centers disappears and the old saying becomes true that you do not fit a uniform to a soldier but a soldier fits his uniform. The play on the athletic fields is incessant. There are obstacle tracks with hurdles to go over and under with high walls to clamber over. Baseball teams sprout from the fields and the tired muscles of the first days are growing firm. The work and play are so hard that food is taken in enormous quantities and the cadet mess has become famous in the whole Army. In many camps officers pay their way to eat at the cadet mess. Milk is consumed in unbelievable amounts. In most messes a quart of milk is placed between each two men for each meal. The cadets are ravenous and the food is good. And very soon the men begin to gain weight. At first they lose the soft flesh, but almost immediately it is replaced with hard, firm flesh and the formations on the drill fields begin to look soldierly. Quickly these young men begin to prove that they are highly selected. They learn the simple formations and the manual of arms much more quickly than the average soldiers. The extra alertness of their minds and bodies responds to training as it might be supposed to. The little overseas caps are worn at a jaunty angle.

By now, the testing and appraising are completed. Perhaps a large proportion of the candidates, actuated by romantic tradition, have asked to be trained as pilots. But the tests have indicated that some would make better navigators and bombardiers. They are assigned to the jobs for which they are best suited. Men in these three positions—pilots, navigators, and bombardiers—will be commissioned when their training is completed. But now they are assigned from the induction centers to the schools which will train them for their highly specialized jobs. Perhaps from the truck which pulls up to the induction center the boy from Idaho will be trained as a bombardier, the university student from Indianapolis has the mathematics and the scholastic background which will make him a good navigator, while the tests have shown that the farmer from South Carolina has the best qualifications for a pilot. Gunners and radio men and engineers will come from another source. They will not be commissioned officers and they need not have either the scholastic training nor the theoretical training required by the other three. It would be impossible to pick out a cadet in the Air Force and say that he is typical of all cadets. There would be no true way of doing this. There is no typical cadet. They are as different, one from another, as any other group of Americans. In spite of some of the poster painting of Arrow Collar pilots, there is no Air Force face or figure. Only two things are typical of cadets—they are above the average mentally and physically. But among them there is nothing typical in economic background, racial stock, or experience. They may come from homes where the father was a working man, a bank clerk, a railroad man, a farmer, a cattle rancher. They may have gone to public or to private schools, to great universities, small colleges, or junior colleges. They need not have been privileged boys in a money sense at all, in fact, most of them are not; but because of their mental endowment they will have done well in school and have had no difficulty with their technical studies. Because of their physical alertness, they will have had considerable training in the team sports of their schools. They will have played football or basketball, have competed in the field or on the track. Many of them will have been ardent hunters and fishermen. Because they are healthy young men they will like girls very well indeed. Because their co-ordination and sense of timing and rhythm is acute, they will generally be good dancers and will like to dance.

Because their ears are highly aware in pitch and range they will like music, and because of all these things they will be good-looking without necessarily being handsome. In their schools, because of their qualities, they will have given evidence of some leadership. They will not be more or less courageous than other young men, but good nervous co-ordination will given them the ability for self-discipline which passes for fearlessness because fear is controlled. Tendencies toward panic or hysteria will have been discovered by the psychological tests they have undergone and the cause found and corrected or the candidate eliminated. In a word the cadets are drawn from a cross-section background of America but they are the top part of the cross section. They represent the best we have.

In training it has been found that boys from farms and from small towns, because of a familiarity with machines and because their individual judgments have oftener been exercised, are a little easier to train for the Air Force, but not enough so that applications from the great cities are not readily accepted. That the cadets are very attractive is easy to demonstrate. Wherever they are posted they very quickly monopolize the time and the thought of the personable young women of the neighborhood.

In trying to assemble a typical bomber crew, one cannot pick a type. The members must be chosen at random. Their training will be identical and rigid, but except for their training they will emerge as officers as individual as they went in; and since, once their training is completed and they are assigned to their units, a great deal of their work will depend on individual judgment, leadership tendencies will be developed in the Air Force rather than stultified by unquestioned orders and control. For it is the principle of the Air Force that men shall know the reasons for orders rather than that they shall obey blindly and perhaps stupidly. Discipline is in no way injured by such an approach. In fact, it is made more complete, for a man can eventually trust orders he understands. The cadets are instructed now and assigned to their positions. They are ready for their individual training.

THE BOMBARDIER

BILL was born and grew up in Idaho. His father was a railroad engineer and their home was a comfortable one. In the town where they lived the family was liked and respected. Bill's father was a product of the alert democracy of the West. His job was dignified and his position in his town and in the Railroad Brotherhood was the result of a sober, controlled life. Bill's mother belonged to the Altar Guild of the Episcopal Church and was a permanent member of the local Red Cross.

When Bill was ten his mother got him started with piano lessons. These continued for two years and came to nothing, but they laid an important groundwork for Bill. In high school he took up the trumpet to the horror of his whole neighborhood, but before long he played well. He organized a little dance orchestra and played for country dances, and when he went to college he was able to make his own way playing in a dance band. In high school Bill's scholastic record was not wonderful but his grades were adequate and could have been better if he had wished, but he was having a series of soul-rocking love affairs and hadn't really time for grades. His favorite subjects were physics and chemistry. He played a good forward on his basketball team and he graduated nicely and without honors.

In the American tradition he took two years then to roam about working at what he could get. He played in a barnstorming orchestra and worked on a hay bailer, but the depression was on and even odd jobs were not easy to get. At length he went to college like many other American boys, to mark time until the depression was over. There was a sense that at least at

47

school one wasn't standing completely still. Bill borrowed a little money to get started and he was lucky about getting into the orchestra. And again his grades were not remarkable but they kept him in school. Bill was entering his fourth year when Pearl Harbor was attacked. He and his friends had wondered vaguely what they would do when they graduated, go on W.P.A. or try to keep the orchestra going, and then Pearl Harbor was attacked and war was declared.

There was a long train trip to the induction center and the ride on the truck and the examinations and tests, and now Bill was ready to begin his training as a bombardier. He was not very tall—5 ft. 7 in. His face was square and firm and his hair sandy. He had cultivated a manner of good-humored taciturnity not very unlike his father's manner. "When you get the feel of it," his father wrote, "I'd like to come down and see what kind of an Air Force we've got."

During the first days, sometimes Bill was a little panicky. He had thought of himself as being pretty hard but now new, sore muscles soon showed him he was not. If he had not been so tired those first few days the constant supervision would have frightened him, but when he was finally released he dropped on his cot and went to sleep. He wrote an occasional post card home. At first he had thought of writing long, descriptive letters to a girl he knew, but he soon gave that up. Things were happening to him too fast for description. He took his aptitude test in a half-bewildered state and he was assigned to a bombardier school. He was to learn a complicated trade and technique in twelve weeks. The program was exact; it went as follows:

1. The objective—proficiency as a bombardier member of the Air Force combat team with a minimum of tactical transition training after the completion of this course.

2. The scope—
   a. Qualification in the technical duties of a bombardier.
   b. Qualification as third-class bombardier.
   c. Qualification in the technical duties of aircraft observer.
   d. Physical training to develop and maintain the alertness required in combat crew members.
   e. Military training to inculcate an appreciation of strict compliance with instructions from higher authority.
3. The duration—12 weeks.
   a. First three weeks preliminary ground training.
   b. 4th to 9th weeks inclusive, ground and air training.
   c. 10th to 12th weeks inclusive, air training to include tactical bombing and reconnaissance missions.

And at the bottom of the program it said, "The hours prescribed herein per phase of instruction represent the time required for the average student to accomplish the objective."

These were the things he had to learn in twelve weeks. Bill, with a number of others from his induction center, were moved to a bombing school. In the barracks he had his own cot now and a little domain about him. He began to make friends and gradually what had seemed like anarchy to him began to iron out. Drill and athletics went on constantly and Bill's shoulders were back now and he began to fit his uniform. At night he was not as tired as he had been at first.

At first he had disliked the formations, but as he became precise in his step and carriage he grew to like them; the beat of the step, the numbers of men all acting in precise unison, became a satisfying thing to him. He discovered something he had not learned, which the directionless depression had not permitted him to learn—the simple truth that concerted action of a group of men produces a good feeling in all of them. In formation he with the others shouted the step count at the top of his lungs and they felt all good about it. When his unit was good enough so that every rifle grounded with one sound, they felt good about that too. They took pride in their unison.

The days were balanced for them, formation to breakfast, and classroom and athletics, then application of the classroom work and more drill and lunch, then back to classroom, out to the formation and practice with appliances. There was so much to do that the days raced by.

The study began in the classroom. There was a discussion of the reason of training, what it aimed toward, and what the duties and the responsibilities of a bombardier are—and his responsibilities are very sharp. He must not only have in his possession many confidential documents, but also he must guard and protect and in a final emergency destroy the secret bombsight. This bombsight has become the symbol of responsibility. It is never left unguarded for a moment. On the ground it is kept in a safe and under constant guard. It is taken out of its safe only by a bombardier on mission and he never leaves it. He is responsible not only for its safety but for its secrecy. And finally, should his ship be shot down, he has been instructed how quickly and effectively to destroy it. The bombardier goes always armed when he has the sight. His mission starts at the moment when he receives the sight from the safe. Instructions for protecting the bombsight are so exact that they amount to a ritual. Discussion of the sight with an unauthorized person is forbidden and no unauthorized person is ever permitted to see it. Packed in its canvas case, it is never even opened except in a guarded classroom, a trainer center, or in the nose of a bomber.

These things were explained on that first day in class and then, after a searching questionnaire, Bill and the others signed certificates of responsibility and were issued their secret textbooks and their equipment.

Now the work was given to them quickly. They discussed the

theory of falling bodies, speed, trajectory, and the variables which affect the fall of a bomb, such as drift of plane and wind. Range problems were given to the class and immediately problems were set down to be worked out by the cadets in the light of their growing knowledge, for no principle is ever given without an immediate application. Thus, the discussion of trajectories is immediately demonstrated with models.

The work was given to them very rapidly. It was poured on, in fact—discussion and demonstration of gyroscopes and finally the bombsights themselves. From classroom they went to drill, from drill to athletics, and always they ate hugely. Now, the bombsights were brought into the classroom and taken apart so that the cadets knew every piece and how it worked, and what they learned cannot be told.

Bill's class had not been off the ground yet, but it was beginning to study the ships. They were taught how to use the oxygen equipment in high altitudes, how to use parachutes. They went into the bombers and learned about the emergency exits and the fire extinguishers.

Bill wrote to his father saying "I don't know how we are going to do it all in twelve weeks. It seems like a mountain ahead, but the others did it so I guess we can. But don't come down here now," he went on; "I don't know whether I could get a moment to see you."

The others not only had done it, but were doing it. There were classes in all degrees of completeness and one class finishing every week. Going to his classrooms, Bill could see the advanced students marching to the training planes—the AT-11's —to fly on practice bombing missions, and at night the planes roared overhead on night missions. The whole field was alive with energy but Bill's class had come to the use of the ground trainer. This was a fascinating gadget, a three-wheel carriage, very tall. It had three seats on the top of it twelve feet above

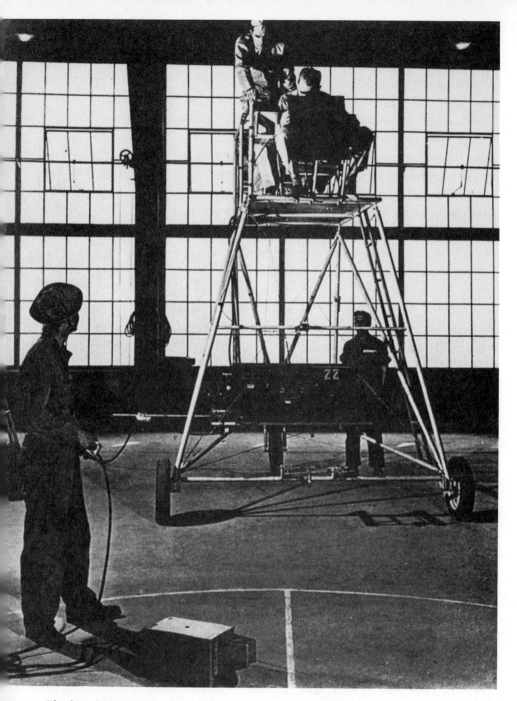

The bombsight trainer

the floor. There were two seats ahead and one behind. The cadet sat in the left-hand seat and his instructor beside him, while the pilot who steered the carriage sat behind. A bombsight was mounted in front of the cadet. Ahead of the carriage, on the floor, a tiny little wagon moved and it had on its flat top a paper target. It was called a bug. It crawled in any set direction. The big carriage moved slowly ahead and the bug moved sideways, but the speed of the carriage was, in relation to the bug, what a bomber's speed would be at high altitudes. The sideways-moving bug simulated the side drift of the plane. Bill sat in his seat looking through the bombsight and he directed the pilot as he would in a plane. He found his target in the bombsight, turned his knobs, correcting for speed and drift, and when he had set the sight to release the bombs his instructor checked his work. Now the carriage was moving over the bug. The sight was set and if Bill's work had been accurate, a plunger in the bottom of the carriage sprang down and punched a hole in the target. After each run the score that Bill made was tabulated on his record. The trainer simulated exactly the conditions of bombing, except for one thing—the trainer did not bounce and buck the way a bomber does in rough air, but it allowed constant use and practice with the bombsight in the reading of dials and scales. With every run over the bug, Bill's scores grew better and he came consistently closer to the bull's eye. Every day he put in an hour on the trainer. His hands were finding the knobs without his looking and his eyes were going automatically to the proper dials. And every day the work in the classroom continued and the drill continued and the athletics continued. In class he was learning bombsighting technique and he was studying the mechanism of the bomb rack. Daily the problems grew more difficult but what seemed impossible of mastery on looking ahead in the textbook, fell into place when he came to it.

Up to this time he had been studying only equipment and the use of it. But now he began to learn his duties in relation to other members of the crew—the nature of the bombing mission, his relation to the pilot, and his co-ordination with the other members of the crew. And he was learning the use of other instruments besides the bombsight, the instruments and their calibration, the air-speed indicator, altimeter, compass, and free-air thermometer. He learned their errors and the corrections. It was not until the twentieth day of his training that he went into the air.

On the morning of Bill's twentieth day, his echelon went to class and learned about low-altitude bombing procedure and how it is different from high-altitude bombing. Every member of the class was excited. The sound of the planes warming up on the flying lines had a new meaning to them. Bill had flown before in commercial ships but there is something very different in an Army ship. The commercial airliner, padded, sound-proofed, uses only straight and level flight. The closed and locked doors of the pilot's compartment, the low, level flying, with gum to chew and aspirin and Amytal for air sickness, the little windows, the leisurely speed, these are not like Army flying. Here is no padding or soundproofing. The AT-11's are noisy. The little seats have no backs. You sit on your parachute and if you are sick, you clean it up yourself.

The orders for Bill's echelon said "Dry Run," that is, they were to run over the target, use the bombsight, but drop no bombs. The instructors would know within a margin how accurate the sighting was. After their lunch Bill's echelon marched out to the flight line. They were only to go to seven thousand feet, so they did not need sheepskins. They were dressed in the flight coveralls and their little caps. The parachutes were issued and each man adjusted the harness to fit him and all of them pretended at nonchalance. Bill leaned against the wall by the

Bombardier cadet carrying the bombsight to his plane

Operations Office, his face a little stern. He wasn't frightened but his heart ticked with excitement and his breathing was a little short, but he wasn't going to let the others know because he didn't know they all felt the same way.

Three cadets and an instructor were going in each ship. On the line the twin engines of the AT-11 began to turn over. The echelon lined up and received its orders and marched out to the planes. They were beautiful ships and, being trainers, they were silver. On their sides and on their wings they had the new Air Force insignia, a white star on a blue field. This is more easily seen than the old red-centered star, and besides the red center was very easy to mistake for the Rising Sun of Japan. The greenhouse—transparent, plastic nose of the ship—shone in the sun. Bill and two classmates and their instructor climbed to the door and settled themselves on their parachutes. It is forbidden to take off or to land in the nose of a bomber. If the ship should nose over, a man would be needlessly hurt. Bill loosened the straps of his parachute where they cut into his legs. There is a good feeling about a parachute, a nice feeling of safety. There is only one time when a parachute is hateful. No guardhouse is provided for cadets who have little difficulties with rules, but sometimes an error in judgment will be punished with an order to walk a given post wearing a parachute.

The parachute case hangs out flat, one edge against the buttocks. It shifts from side to side with each step. No care in walking will keep it still. Thus after ten minutes of walking post, the area where it slides becomes a little tender, and in half an hour sore, and at the end of two hours perhaps a line of blisters has formed and the erring cadet has been truly spanked by proxy. Every step is painful and there is no dignity in the pain. Further, in some posts, any cadet can quicken your step simply by whistling "Yankee Doodle" in a tempo faster than you are walking and you are required to keep step with his whistling.

56

Gradually your parachute ceases to be your friend and becomes your executioner.

In the plane the metal door slammed shut and, waiting in turn in the line, the bombing trainer moved out and taxied to the runway. The three cadets adjusted their safety belts and their eyes found each other's eyes and they smiled a little self-consciously. The ship bounced and rattled along. The metal walls did not turn aside the noise of the motors. Bill sat rigidly on his little seat. Then the plane stopped and in turn the motors roared and then the brakes were released. Bill saw the pilot push both the red knobs of his throttles far ahead. Bill's weight was threefold against his back as the ship rushed down the runway, and then it lifted gently and the noise of motor and vibration became less. Bill felt rather than saw the steep turn and they leveled away toward the bombing range. The instructor motioned him forward. He clambered to his feet and edged his way between the empty bomb racks. He climbed past the co-pilot's feet, down into the nose. From his seat he could see in all directions, up and down and sideways, and by leaning over he could even see down in back. He was suspended over a slowly moving world. The bombsight was in front of him. The seat and position were familiar to him because of the ground trainer. Automatically his hand went out to the microphone of the communication system and draped it by its cord over his knee. The instructor nodded approval. On the trainer there had been a dummy microphone of wood hung on a rope. It was there so the cadets would automatically use it from the first. Bill settled his head phones down over his ears and plugged into the system. They were flying at seven thousand feet now. Far ahead Bill could see the target on the ground, three concentric circles, and in the center a little white building which was the bull's eye—his first dry run over his first target. The instructor's voice was loud in his ears, "Take over the run." Bill was frightened. He looked

57

Bombardier cadet looks through his bombsight at the target just ahead

into his sight and found his target. He checked altitude and drift and in the microphone he called directions to the pilot. He was amazed that he knew what to do and that it worked. He felt that a great deal depended on his first run. His face was tight and his lips pinched as he worked the knobs. He heard the instructor say "Relax, you'll burn yourself out." The target was ahead and drifting near when he set his release. He lifted his phone to his lips and for the first time in a moving plane he shouted "Bombs away." The instructor squinted through the sight just before the release and he nodded and picked up his phone. "Try another from the northwest," he said.

When Bill came back from his first dry run he climbed out of the plane feeling much older than when he had gone. His parachute bounced on him impudently. He hadn't dropped a single bomb yet, but he had found a target on the ground on the crossed hairs of a bombsight. It was his first little graduation and he felt very good about it. He felt so good about it that he and another cadet took a bus to town that evening. They had not been away from the camp since they had come to the bombardier school, and once out of the camp, standing on the street, they felt deserted and lonely. Civilians looked strange to them, even a little funny. Bill had never noticed clothes very much, but now his eyes saw how many colors in neckties there were and he looked at shirts and cuts of civilian clothes and hats and they seemed odd and outlandish.

Before he had been in the Army he had not noticed girls in great detail. There were pretty ones and homely ones, well- and badly-dressed ones. He had lumped them in generalities, but now it was nearly a month since he had see any girl and his eyes noticed things he had not seen before—how differently they were made, how differently they walked, and he saw expressions that he had never seen before. But mostly he felt alone and unprotected. He and his companion walked along the street and

59

looked in store windows. They bought some post cards and addressed and mailed them. On a corner there was a little beer and dancing place, a bar, a small dance floor, a juke box, and some tables. They went in and ordered beer and sat down. It was a very gaudy place. After a while they danced with some girls and talked to them. They forgot the time.

It was Bill's first run-in with military law. On the record sheet in his squadron room, three gold stars were pasted opposite his name and for each star he contributed 50 cents to the squadron fund; and the next evening Bill and his friend walked post for three hours, a hundred yards up and a hundred yards back. Their parachutes jerked about and rubbed tender places on their backs. Back and forth they marched for three hours. And Bill heard in his ears again the captain's voice, "It may remind you to look at your watch," and when Bill said lamely, "I did, sir, but my watch must have been wrong," the answer was final, "There are no wrong watches in the Air Forces. There are no excuses," the captain went on. "We're not trying to baby you. You're going to be an officer. You'll have to control yourself. That is your responsibility. You can do what you want in your free time but you must obey the rules." And he added, "Just a little advice. Don't ever use that wrong-watch business again. That doesn't bring out the best in me or in anyone else. Three hours to walk post."

Bill felt disgraced. He walked dolefully back and forth with the parachute banging behind. In the morning he was not only sleepy, but very sore.

No one seemed to remember his disgrace afterward. It was over and done with. Classwork continued with more work on the trainer and dry runs over the target every day. Bill was getting used to the equipment and his scores were getting better. Now a new process was started.

In the mornings he and his echelon went out to the skeet

range. With 12-gauge shotguns they fired at the little clay plates that came flying out of the towers. Instruments are only as valuable as a good eye makes them. The skeet shooting developed timing and lead.

In class they studied the nature of errors in bombing, errors due to variation in altitude, speed, and drift, and how to compute the amount of these errors in feet. And on the ranges they practiced shooting a .45-caliber automatic pistol.

On the twenty-third day, Bill dropped his first practice bombs. These are built exactly like real 100-pound bombs. They are metal shells and they are filled with sand. They weigh exactly one hundred pounds. In the tail of the bomb there is a little bomb of black powder and a firing pin to set it off when it hits the ground. There is not much explosive force in a practice bomb, but it makes a flash at night and a gray smoke in the daytime and it makes a loud bang. The cameras which record the scores and photograph the smoke or the flash create a permanent bombing record on film. Now, every day, Bill went on actual bombing missions over the target and the bomb bays were open when he ran in to the target. Before the take-off he inspected the blue-painted practice bombs slung on the racks and in flight he pulled the safety pins. There are two pins on a bomb—one, a cotter pin, is removed when the ship is in the air, but the bomb still cannot fire for its other pin is a wire, one end of which is fastened to the bomb rack and this one is pulled out automatically when the bomb falls free.

Now Bill had something really to drop on the target. As he made his approach, the bomb bays were opened; he found his mark, made his corrections, and set his release and then the bomb scraped metallically as it was released. It seemed to hang in the air under the plane for a moment, trailing horizontally, and then slowly it nosed over and began its curving flight toward the target. The bomb struck and a flash and a puff of

61

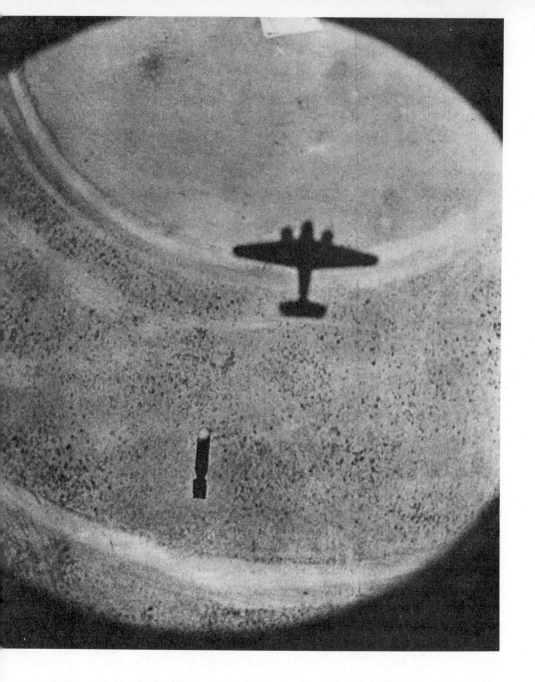

Falling bomb and the plane's shadow approaches the target

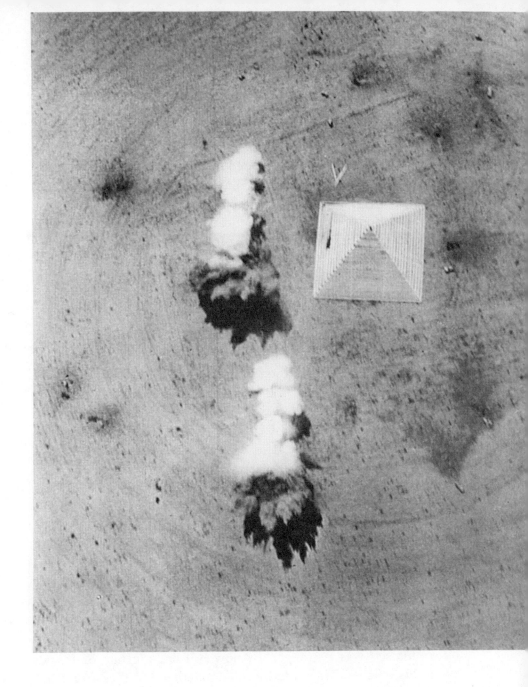

The cadet achieves a near miss

smoke showed the score. He dropped single bombs with the wind and against the wind and in cross winds, checked his results on his score sheet. And he learned to drop trains of bombs, that is, evenly spaced so that a line of explosions walked over the target. And he dropped salvos, that is, all the bombs in one rack falling at once. The practice was constant.

In the classroom the echelon began the study of tactics, the reasons for formations. They learned the difference in objectives and what effective weight of bombs would be necessary to destroy different objectives. The training went beyond actual bombing. They learned the use of aerial cameras, maps, map reading. They studied codes and ciphers and the shapes and insignias of all planes. With models, they learned to identify the aircraft of other nations, both of our Allies and our enemies. Classwork, athletics, and bombing practice went on every day. They studied meteorology, clouds and fog, air current, smoke, haze, and dust. All of the changes in the air which may affect aircraft were considered and they are very many: icing conditions, rain, snow, mist, sleet, hail, together with the condition of the air before and after each one—thunderstorms and air turbulence. The weeks were running away rapidly. The class was given a short course in basic navigation with the principles of taking bearings.

Bill bombed a lighted target at night and sometimes a low-flying plane dropped powerful flares on parachutes over a dark target and Bill bombed from a higher altitude.

Bill was becoming a bombardier but he was becoming a soldier too. His walk had changed and his posture. It seemed years since he had been a civilian, so long that he could hardly remember how it was. The person who got up late and had days to himself was a stranger. By now Bill had a group of friends in his echelon. They went to town together and they didn't forget the time. They had met some girls with whom they danced and had dinner in their free time. Bill was hard now, his muscles didn't hurt any more. He had gained ten pounds. The time was coming close for his graduation as a bombardier and his commissioning.

On the bombing range he worked in formations of planes. The missions became more exact and the tactical problems more complex. He studied gunnery and went out to the firing range to shoot at moving targets with a machine gun, for the bombardier must operate the gun in the nose of his ship and protect that area from attack. Every day the work in the classroom became more technical. His echelon learned to recognize surface ships, battleships, aircraft carriers, cruisers, destroyers. With models they learned what Japanese ships looked like and Italian and German ships. They studied depth bombs and how they are used on submarines, and the newspaper reports of bombing raids began to have a new meaning. Bill knew now the problems involved in sending five hundred bombers over Germany, the complicated supply, the rendezvous, the split-second arrival over the target, and the dispersal to little fields again. And when a Japanese fleet was attacked and beaten at Midway Island by bombers which had come a long way, Bill could see in the light of his training how it had been done.

He was still flying in training ships. His experience in the big ships, the Fortresses and the B-24's, would come when he became bombardier of a permanent crew. As the cadets hardened physically and became more disciplined mentally, the work was given to them more and more quickly. On the sixty-sixth day of their training the squadron marched to inspection. They were not much like the sprawling boys who had stumbled off the trucks at the induction center.

In Bill's echelon they had talked of what they would do when they graduated, of the tremendous party they would have. They thought of the time when the eagle would be on their caps and the bars on their shoulders and the weight of the bombardier's wings over the left-hand breast pocket. One or two of them had uniform catalogues, all marked up. That was going to be the great time when they graduated and were commissioned. They had planned for it very carefully, and on the seventy-second day of their training it happened. In spite of their planning it crept up on them. The squadron was graduated. They were bombardiers in the Army Air Force.

Bill had planned to ask his father to come down for it, but he hadn't. There was too much work to do. There is a sense of hurry over everything. The nation is at war. There isn't time for ceremony and parade. This isn't a war of flags and marching. It is a war of finding the target in the cross hairs of the bombsight and setting the release, and it isn't a war of speeches and frothy hatred. It is a technical job, a surgeon's job. There is only time for hatred among civilians. Hatred does not operate a bombsight.

Bill did not invite his father to his graduation. He was to go to a camp where the bomber crews are assembled and trained as units and he had a week's leave. He went home. And out of some kind of diffidence he didn't even tell his father and mother he was coming. Instead, he got off the train at two in the afternoon and he walked to his home. His father looked at him and then looked quickly away. "We've always been a fighting family," he said. His mother asked "How much time have you?" "A week," said Bill. And his father said, "Bill, would you like to go fishing, would you?"

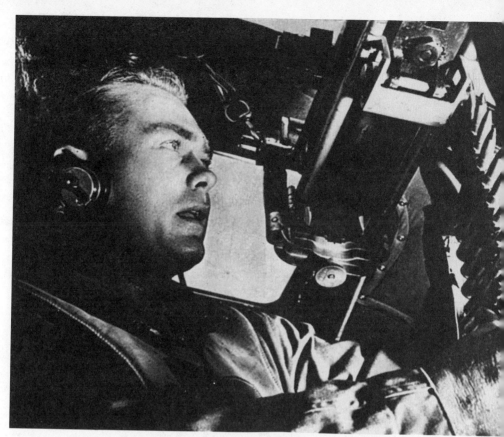

Bombardier loads the machine gun in the nose of a bomber

THE AERIAL GUNNER

THE gunners of the United States Army Air Force will go into our military history with a tradition for toughness and versatility and courage. The aerial gunner of a bomber should be small because the turrets and the tail section where he takes his post are small. The pony express riders were about the only comparable group that we know. The riders too had to be small so that they could carry more mail and at the same time protect

Aerial gunner practicing with a flexible gun mount

their horses. The aerial gunner at his best, is a slender, short, wiry young man with stringy muscles, a deadly eye, and no nerves. His trade is one of the few in the world where a good little man is a great deal better than a good big man.

Sitting in the turret of a bomber, with his hands on the controls of his turret and on the trigger of his two .50-caliber machine guns, the gunner is bigger than anything he can hit. Of aerial gunnery, General Arnold says in *Winged Warfare*, "This is strictly a military specialty. There is no civil counterpart. It appeals to the old soldier type who likes a trigger in his hand and who likes to feel the power and effect of the whistle of the machine gun bullet and the smooth operation of the machine gun or cannon.

"The machine gunner is a combat crew member on multiple speedy fighters, observation and reconnaissance aircraft and he is of special importance on all types of bombardment, light, medium and heavy. Some gunners will operate .30- or .50-caliber guns, each firing at the rate of over six hundred rounds per minute. Others will operate the slower firing 20 mm. and 37 mm. guns with a bigger kick. Upon the shoulders of this air specialist rides the safety of the plane while in flight in areas infested by hostile pursuit. In combat, the skill, coolness and courage of the aerial gunner spell the safety of the big bomber and may provide the sole means of saving this quarter million dollar vessel and its valuable human cargo from destruction and ensure the completion of its mission."

There are advantages in a small man beyond his ability to fit comfortably in the turret. A small man is usually quicker than a big man. In the ring a bantamweight fighter moves faster than a heavyweight, but in the ring the little man can rarely deliver a knockout punch to a big man. In a bomber, with the .50-caliber guns under his hand, the little man suffers no such deficiency. He can knock anything out of the air that flies, big or

69

little. Like the pony express rider, great responsibilty is in his hands. In a bomber the gunner's position is said to be defensive and it is true that the gunner rarely moves to attack, but it is hard to see how shooting Zeros out of the air could be called defensive. Perhaps it could be said that the gunner attacks defensively.

In our young Air Force the aerial gunner has already become a legendary figure. The stories told about him are very many. The most recent one is of a tail gunner who did not report shooting down three Japanese planes because he had not had orders to fire.

It is strange how the tradition of a post takes hold of a man and molds him. The ideal gunner, as has been said, is a small, wiry man of cold courage. The gunners are probably the cockiest group in the whole Army. They walk on their toes and are not offered, nor will they take, any nonsense. They are non-commissioned officers. They draw extra pay, but actually their position and rating in the Air Force has little to do with chevrons or pay. They are respected and needed out of all proportion to their purely military rating. They are the executioners of the air.

They soon get a great sense of their importance in the service, and they carry their importance with dignity. They are a cool, cocky, efficient lot, and it is not a good idea to trifle with a little man who wears the insignia of an aerial gunner. He has been picked for his coolness, speed, and accuracy and spirit. He is the stinger in the tail of the long-range bomber. A crew with good gunners feels itself very fortunate. Of course every member of a bomber crew is trained to operate the guns but the gunner is the true expert. Already the trail of wrecked Japanese fighters is a proof of his efficiency and, although his discipline is rigid, in flight and in combat, the safety of the great ship depends on his judgment and his aim.

70

The aerial gunner will emerge from this war with a reputation not unlike that of the Texas Ranger, but with this exception—he will be the good little man who is better than the good big man. As with other members of the bomber crew, it is found that Americans with the American tradition are peculiarly apt at becoming good gunners.

Wing Commander C. E. Beamish of the Royal Air Force at Harlingen as liaison officer between British and U. S. aerial forces, in gunnery training, has said about the excellence of American gunners, "The average boy in the States has fired a gun before. He has used a gun a lot compared to the boy in England."

The use of any kind of gun helps to develop a gunner. The kids with BB guns are developing the gunner's eye, a sense of lead and trajectory, the almost instinctive technique of gunnery. All the knowledge and reading in the world will not take the place of practice.

In the Air Force there are the best trapshooters in the world acting as instructors in gunnery. These champion shots agree that guns are guns; that a boy who can hit a clay pigeon on a skeet range can knock a Messerschmitt out of the air. And nearly all boys in America have a feeling for firearms fathered by the American tradition and developed by the toys which shoot rubber-tipped arrows, through air rifles, to .22's and shotguns. Boys with such training make excellent aerial gunners. They know the whole basis of gunnery before they start to work with a flexible machine gun. You do not have to teach such a boy not to fire point-blank at a moving plane. He has learned to lead a moving target shooting duck and quail. He knows the principles of sighting and of deflection and of trajectory, but he doesn't even know he knows them for he learned them with a single-shot .22 shooting ground squirrels at extreme range.

71

It is not at all a matter of boasting to say that we are a nation of gunners. It is demonstrated by the speed with which the gunnery schools turn out aerial gunners and the deadly accuracy of those gunners. There are already Paul Bunyans among our gunners and there will be more. Nothing quite like the American aerial gunner has been seen on the face of the earth, but he is a natural descendent of the Kentucky hunter and the Western Indian-fighter. With the tradition of the frontiersman in his blood and a new weapon in his hand the American boy simply changes the nature of his game. Instead of raiding Sioux or Apache, instead of buffalo and antelope, he lays his sights on Zero or Heinkel, on Stuka or Messerschmitt. The weapon is basically the same as that which his father and his grandfather used. It fires a bigger slug faster and farther and more rapidly. His projectile will pierce armor plate, but a gun barrel and human eye and spirit have not much changed since any of them came into being.

Our gunner material is the best there is. It remains only to put it through the training which will make it best able to use the modern weapons.

The candidates for gunner school are either enlisted men or men who enlist in the Air Force giving aerial gunnery as their preference. They must pass the same rigid physical examination cadets do, but they need not have the technical education that cadets must have. But their eyes and nerves and bodies must be perfect. Under tests, their judgment, their sense of distance and of timing must show as excellent, and they must have this recommendation from their squadron commanders, "I would be willing for this man to serve as gunner on the plane which I pilot in combat." This is a very special kind of recommendation, for it means that the pilot is trusting his blind and vulnerable side to the safekeeping of this particular young man.

The boys who go into the service volunteer for aerial gunnery for only one reason—they want to take part in action, and it is one very sure way of seeing action. A pilot or a navigator might be assigned to Ferrying Command, to freight or passenger carrying, but the gunner has only one purpose—to shoot enemy planes out of existence. Where he goes there is going to be action. Thus his Service attracts the real fighting men of the country, not those who want protection and desk work, but the men with the fighting blood and spirit that have made the country. Your gunner is the real thing. His insignia means action. As one gunner said, "Hell, that is what I got into the ——war for."

There is no doubt about it, gunners are true fighting men—"The type who likes a trigger in his hand." For a while the rumor went around about how dangerous the gunner's job is, but it is no more dangerous than the pilot's job or the bombardier's job, and the safety, not only of the gunner, but of the pilot and navigator too, are in the gunner's hands. He has that advantage over them. If he sees danger approaching in the shape of an attacking plane he has the means in his control to eliminate it. His guns will shoot as fast and as far as anything that comes against him and no American could ask for more advantage than that.

Having been tested, accepted, and assigned, the candidate will be sent to gunnery school. There in five weeks he will be taught his trade and from there he will be assigned to his permanent bomber crew. He will take his place on the team.

The weapons of a long-range bomber are .50-caliber machine guns, mounted in pairs about three feet apart and controlled and fired in unison so that not one line of bullets but two spray at an enemy. While the gunner will be trained to handle the lighter .30-caliber guns, and the heavy 20 mm. and 37 mm. cannon, if he is to be bomber man, the .50-caliber double-barreled flexible guns will be his babies. These are mounted in flexible turrets in

73

the transparent blisters on top of the bomber, in the belly blister under the ship, and in the tail. There is a gun in the nose of the ship, but the bombardier takes care of that.

The gunners are responsible for attack from above, from below, and from the rear. The power-driven turrets move around at a guiding touch of the fingers and the twin guns move up and down with a very light touch. A squeeze on the trigger and the heavy armor-piercing bullets pour out. The whole turret, gunner and all, swings around to face the target.

The training of the gunner in his five weeks is direct. He must learn to fire the various Air Force weapons with accuracy and effectiveness, and he must learn the parts of his guns, how to care for them and how to repair them. He must learn theory and method of fire and ballistics. In addition, he must learn his enemies, the kinds of planes the enemy flies and the methods of attack. He must recognize an enemy plane by its shape and size, for he cannot permit it to come close enough to see its insignia. During his five weeks' training he will fire a great many shots at a great many kinds of targets.

It takes five weeks to train a gunner for a bomber crew. His training will be as it should be—guns and shooting, theory of sighting and lead, but shooting all the time, practice with many different kinds of arms on many kinds of targets, so that the candidate emerges a shooting man who knows and loves and handles his guns. He must be very good, for when his crew finally climbs into a big ship and taxies off to its mission, the belly and back and tail of the ship are in the gunner's hands. On his accurate eye and steady hand depend the lives of the crew, the safety of the ship, and, most of all, the success of the mission.

If a man has loved hunting where he pitted himself, his will, his nerve, and his marksmanship against big game, he could not ask for better sport, for in his shining blister on the back

74

Tail gunner in a power-driven turret of a B–24

of a bomber he will be hunting the biggest game in the world
—the Zeros, the Stukas, the Heinkels, and the Messerschmitts.
Aerial gunners are the number one sportsmen of our time, and
Al is a typical member of this select circle.

Al was a tough little man from a small town in the Middle
West. He was twenty-one years old, five feet five inches tall,
weighed 138 pounds, and he was lean and wiry. He had played
forward on his high school basketball team and shortstop for
the baseball team. He boxed as an amateur and a good many
people had told him he should go professional and make some
money at it. He had cold, blue eyes and a pitcher's face. He had
light hair and a perpetual cowlick.

The times had been hard on him and on his family. When
war broke out Al was jerking sodas in a candy store and not
too happy about it. He joined the Army because it seemed silly
to him to wait to be drafted and he joined the Air Force because it offered the kind of action he felt he wanted. The soda
fountain had put a brand on him, because he thought of himself as a man of action. His reading was dominated by adventure stories and hunting stories. Before the war, his ideal dream
future had been going to the Aleutian Islands and hunting
Kodiak bears.

Al was proud of his speed in action and of his strength for
his size. He could beat a straight pin-ball game, and when he
worked at the soda fountain he kept himself in condition with
a set of bar bells. He liked to astonish people, who, seeing how
small he was, thought he was also weak.

In the Air Force he went through his preliminary training,
and when he heard about the openings for aerial gunners he
did not hesitate for a moment. It seemed to him his kind of a
job. He was gunner material. He was small, he was tough, and
he wanted action.

Ground service did not appeal to him. He wanted to fly and he wanted to shoot.

After his application and examination, his commanding officer felt the same way about it. He recommended Al for gunnery and the assignment came through and Al was sent to an Army Air Force gunnery school.

It was a big school where Al went. The newly built barracks stretched out in all directions and it was in a desolate place, in desert country; for with so much firing, it is just as well if not much civil population lives in the area. Projectiles from .50-caliber, 20 mm. and 37 mm. guns travel a long distance. The districts near the ranges were restricted to Army personnel.

Every week in the school a new class started and every week a class finished. As in every other branch of the Air Force, no time was wasted. Classwork started immediately, but it was not technical classwork. An instructor lectured, but there were guns and ammunition in front of him for demonstration. The first things to learn were the standard guns of the Air Force: the flexible .30- and .50-caliber machine gun, that is, the movable guns which are aimed at a moving target by the gunner; and the fixed guns—the 20 mm. and 37 mm. rapid-firing cannon which are rigid in the plane and are aimed by aiming the whole ship.

The instructor lectured to the new class and he demonstrated with the guns. Al learned each part of each gun, what its name is and what its purpose is. He learned to take the guns to pieces and to reassemble them. The lessons included the things which may go wrong with a gun and how to rectify the stoppage of fire. The class learned about magazines, their care and handling and stowage. They learned different types of ammunition, armor-piercing, tracers, high explosives, and what each type is designed for and what it will do, how far and how fast it travels.

77

A gunner receiving instructions in skeet shooting

The class handled the ammunition and learned to identify each kind, and when they knew the guns they learned how they are installed in the ships and how the ammunition is stowed. At the end of the first phase of training, they knew every part of the gun, had watched the principles of firing and recoil, of loading and ejection, and when each day's work was done the class had its athletics—volleyball and basketball and baseball.

At a gunnery school there is constant practice. The compressed air BB guns were in use all the time. There is a shooting gallery, only very much larger than any private shooting gallery. Mounted at intervals are little machine guns which operate by compressed air. They fire streams of BB shot at moving targets.

78

The targets are little planes which move rapidly across a blue background but when they are hit, they fall backwards. These guns are in use all the time. The gunners are encouraged to use them whenever they are free, and although the little guns do not fire at very high velocity, nor do the planes move very fast, the constant shooting of these guns develops the shooter's eye, makes him aware of a moving target and how to lead 'it. He learns here too not to fire a constant stream and let the plane run into it, but to fire in bursts so that each shot takes effect.

It is said that when the gunnery students go to town they head first for a shooting gallery to shoot at ducks and moving pipes and clown's heads, that they spend their money on cartridges in private shooting galleries.

Shooting is not only the business of the gunnery school, but its sport too. Even the girls who work in the offices take their places in the shooting galleries. There are other kinds of shooting beyond the use of military weapons. The Air Force has developed an extension of the photo-electric cell shooting which is now in all penny arcades. With these a moving shadow plane is shot down by electricity but the weapon aimed is an actual machine gun. Probably the shotgun training is the best non-military shooting the student gunner has. A man who can hit a moving target with a shotgun, can bring down an enemy plane.

Al's class started with simple trapshooting. They moved from station to station while the little clay plates flew always in the same direction. But soon they took up skeet shooting and in this they never knew which way the target would fly. But instructors stood behind them, showed them how to stand, how to aim, how far to fire ahead of a cross flying target, a target moving away or rising or falling. The instruction was good but only by constant practice could the class achieve the instant judgment of lead and timing so that they began to break the targets in the air. This was Al's meat. His scores improved every

79

On the skeet range

day. He had the quick eye and fast reaction time of a natural gunner and he had the liking for his work which kept him at it.

Toward the end of their training they were given the sport-ingest trapshooting in the world. This is an invention of the Air Force and has never been used by civilians. The shooter sits in a swivel seat on the back of a truck. The road he travels is purposely rough so that he is jiggled and shaken about. As the truck passes each one of sixteen dugouts a target flies and the marksmen must try to hit it. And not only is the truck moving and bouncing, but no two of the traps throw the target in the same direction, nor at the same level. The man who can break

Firing at clay pigeons from a moving base

a good score on this course is really a trapshooter. But the course was not established for fun. It is one thing to fire from a fixed and steady base at a moving target and quite another to fire from a moving base, for here are two speeds which must be calculated, your own and the target's, and if your base is jiggling too, you have three problems. And these are the problems of an aerial gunner flying in rough air and firing at an attacking plane.

The trapshooting experts of the country are enthusiastic about this training technique and the gunners improve every day. It is their improvement which demonstrates whether they are gunners or not. Al's first trip on the course gave him two hits out of sixteen, his second day, five hits; and then he settled down to a good consistent eleven out of sixteen which is championship shooting. He felt that he had found his place. There was no word here about his smallness. He was the ideal size for a gunner and he had the eye and nerve and cockiness of a gunner.

At work his uniform was the loose one-piece coverall of the Air Force and a small cap with a long visor like a baseball cap, which pilots also use because it shades the eyes without getting in the way and because you can wear ear phones over it.

In the classroom they studied tactical firing and controlled fire and they learned the gunner's responsibility to the ship, the crew, and the mission. And now models and silhouettes of the airplanes of the world were brought out and the class was taught through practice to recognize the ships by length and shape of wing, by engine mount, and from every possible angle. This recognition is very important. One must know as far off as possible whether a ship is friend or enemy and if one makes a mistake it may be too late. The class memorized the plane types so that they could call out nationality and type after a one-second look at the silhouette.

And now they knew the guns, and they began to study the gun sights, to know sighting errors and how to correct them. And they studied relative movement and where to fire if a target is coming toward you or crossing or moving away. They worked with a camera gun, learning to estimate speed and relative speed. At last they were ready to fire the machine guns from fixed mounts. Trucks carried the class out to the firing range where the guns were set up on standards. The first training was fire at a fixed target at 200 yards and at 500 yards.

The scoring method was ingenious. Cartridge tips are dipped in colored paint, blue or red or green or yellow. Each man has his own color, and where the bullet hits the target it leaves a little of the paint so that each man can find the hits he has made.

The next problem was firing at a moving target. Ahead of the gun there is an embankment about eight feet high and behind it lies a railroad track which runs in a large triangle. On this track a car runs carrying a cloth target on a rigging. From the guns the car cannot be seen nor hit, but the target slips along in sight. By running around the triangles the target presents different angles for the guns and thus different speeds in relation to the guns. Thus if it is traveling at an angle away from the fire, its speed in relation to the gun will be less than when it travels at right angles to the line of fire. To get the men used to firing at a moving target they first used .22 automatic rifles, but soon they graduated to .30-caliber machine guns and to .50-caliber machine guns.

It is the tendency of most novices to fire great numbers of shots, perhaps hoping that one will hit the target, and it is a matter of discipline to fire short bursts—in a word, to shoot a machine gun like a rifle and not like a fire hose.

It was hot on the firing range, but under a tented cover were cans of water, kept cool by wet cloths wrapped around them. Each man was assigned a certain number of shells to fire at the target under different circumstances every day.

On the firing range, Al loaded a belt of cartridges into the .30-caliber machine gun as he had been taught in class. The very tips of his bullets had been dipped in red paint. He took the gun in his hands and felt for the trigger. His instructor stood close behind him, looking over his shoulder. Al looked through the rear ring sight and found the front sight in the circle, and he braced himself for the firing of the gun.

His instructor said, "Look, you have been shooting a shotgun, you expect this thing to kick. Well, it won't. The recoil action takes up all of the kick. Now, get your eye closer to that sight or you can't see your target." Al leaned close to his sight

On the machine gun range

and put his front sight on the white target 500 yards away. The trigger had a long pull. He squeezed it gently and the rattle of .30-caliber bullets poured out of the gun. In spite of instruction he had braced so hard that on his first burst he missed the target. The empty brass cases rattled out of the right-hand side of the gun and it didn't kick. He drew another bead on the target and this time he didn't flinch. The first time you fire a machine gun, you have the feeling that it has got away from you and you can't stop it; but gradually you learn to release pressure on the trigger almost as soon as you have made contact, thus causing the gun to fire in little short bursts of five to ten shots. All down the line of the range other gunners were firing at the same target. They had all stuffed cotton in their ears, not because the noise is so loud but because it becomes irritating after a while. Each man fired 200 rounds at the fixed target and then they went out and brought in the big square of cloth, laid it on the ground, and found that there were colored holes in the fabric where each bullet had left a little ring of paint around each hit. Some were green and some were red, some were blue, and in this way each man could see the shots he had put in the target.

On the second day on the firing range they did not flinch from the guns any more but they fired at the moving target, the streamer carried by the little car on the triangular track. The target moved straight across their line of fire, then turned and made a run at an angle away from them, turned again and angled in, and behind each man his instructor gave him advice on how far to lead the moving target. Every fifth bullet was a tracer and even in the broad day they could see it drive toward the target. A tracer bullet has a small hole in the rear of the projectile. This hole is filled with calcium which ignites when the bullet is fired so that a brilliant calcium flare shoots from the gun. With tracer bullets you can see how you are shooting and correct your aim. The gunnery class was not very accurate at first, but under the constant supervision of its instructors its scores day by day grew better. Now they were using the principles they had learned on the trapshooting range. You cannot be told how far to lead a moving target, you must simply do it until you know.

In the class they began to study the mechanism and action of the standard gun mount, the waist turret, the bomber turret, the open port mount, the tail gun mount, the tourelle mount, and when they had learned the mechanism of the turret each man was put in to learn to work it. You sit in a small iron seat in a bomber turret, bracing your feet against the foot plate, and there are bars for your hands not unlike the handle bars of a bicycle. Under your urging the whole turret turns either way. The mechanism is driven by an electric battery. A pressure to the right turns the turret to the right. You can make it turn slowly or very rapidly. A slight pressure down on the handle raises the guns and a pressure upward lowers it. The trigger is under your right finger. It is not a technique to be learned easily or quickly. Only practice makes a man proficient. But when he is practiced he can find a target and keep his sight on it as it moves across the sky. Co-ordination of hand and eye must be very acute if one is to operate a turret well. The guns project to right and left on either side of you but your sight is in the middle, cross hairs on a standing glass. It is in the turret that the need for small men as gunners becomes apparent, for the space is crowded. You are surrounded with magazines of ammunition and with the machinery of the turret itself. Over your head is a dome of clear plastic through which you can see in all directions. The turret is a delicate and complex instrument and the mechanics of it are a military secret.

As in all Air Force training, the time at the gunnery school went very quickly. The students were gun-minded young men. They fired on the ranges and they talked firing in the post exchange. In the daily papers they looked for any reference to aerial gunnery in action in Europe, in Australia, or in China; the students were aware of the increasing importance of aerial gunnery. The spirit of their place in the Air Force was beginning to take hold of them. In the barracks Al tried to read his usual adventure stories, but they didn't hold him any more. There was nothing in the magazine that would take the place of the things in his head. He wanted to be a gunner on a long-range bomber, a B-17E or a B-24, and although he didn't tell anyone about it there was a story going on in his head about Al the Gunner over Tokyo or over Berlin. In his mind at night he

Tracer bullets being fired from a power-driven turret

could see his tracers find the vitals of attacking enemy fighters. He knew what it would look like, for he had seen moving pictures of the way a ship staggers when it is killed and noses over and leaps down until it blows up with a puff of black smoke. And in his mind it was Al's guns that were doing these things. It was much better than the stories he had read.

In the classroom they studied tactics of air offense and defense. They learned where an enemy plane attacks from, the angles it will fly at, and they learned where they must fire to bring it down. On moving models the class saw the course a bullet describes between two moving planes, how the bullet curves forward if the planes are parallel and backward if they are flying opposite. They had studied from silhouettes and models the shapes of friend and enemy planes, and now with models and silhouettes they studied the shapes of enemy ships, models of Japanese aircraft carriers, models of Japanese and Italian cruisers. On the firing range they began to work with a .50-caliber machine gun. These guns fire more slowly than the .30's but they have great range and great penetrating quality. The projectile will pierce an inch of armor plate. They look like the .30-caliber guns but they are just bigger all over—bigger and faster.

Al's class went on the range at night and fired tracer bullets at a lighted target and the night was slashed with the lines of the bullets; and all the time the trapshooting went on and the trapshooting from the moving trucks. Eye and hand and judgment were in constant use. They had fired from a fixed base at moving targets now, they had worked the turret and the flexible gun, and at last it was time for them to go into the air. The practice firing would be with a flexible machine gun from an open cockpit plane. The students had learned to load their own belts of ammunition, to take care of their guns. They had learned to repair them when they were broken, how to get them quickly in action when they were jammed, but they had been ground gunners up to now.

On Al's first day in the air he took his gun and mounted it in the plane as he had been taught to do. He was to fire at a target towed by another airplane. He wore goggles and a helmet, for he would have to lean into the fierce wind to fire, and as he settled himself in the rear cockpit he felt strangely competent, for he knew his weapon very well and his firing score had been consistently good.

Before he had got into the plane he had trued his sight, that is, he had laid his guns in a permanent rack and sighted through his sight at a permanent mark. If the sights were not true it

Aero-gunner carrying his ammunition for his first aerial practice

would have showed there. As he had walked out to the plane carrying his gun he had seen a reflection of himself in a window and he had wished that the owner of the candy store where he had jerked sodas could see him now. He felt that everything he had wanted to be was justified. He was a competent little man with a competent big gun. The tow plane took off ahead of him and Al's plane followed. They flew twenty miles to a firing range. Al had his orders and he was to attack, paralleling the target which is called a beam attack. He was to fire at it from various angles coming and going. On the range the tow plane let out the target on its spool until it dragged far behind. The air was not easy. Al's plane jerked and jumped.

Al saw now that it was a great deal more difficult to fire from a moving plane than from a steady place on the ground.

The work on the ground continued, firing of flexible guns on the gunnery range at a moving target, the firing of the cannon and the skeet shooting, but now every day there was aerial training. Every day the silver training ships went up with student gunners in the cockpits. Al fired at the towed target from every angle, from below, from above, and from the sides. He went into high altitudes to attack the target and he wore oxygen mask and heavy sheepskin clothing and gloves; and when the ships landed after firing he went over the target, looking for the marks which would be his hits, and he was graded on the number of his hits.

In the classroom he learned group attack and formation attack on tail and on nose. He fired from the five standard installations, nose, tail, blister, waist turret, and open port, and every day he had his athletics and calisthenics, and every day squadron drill and squadron ceremony. Al had gained confidence in himself now and in his weapon. He was becoming a gunner. He knew every part and symptom of his gun. His eye could calculate the speed of moving objects. His hands on the guiding levers of the turret moved instinctively.

With so much to do and so much to learn, the weeks moved quickly by. It seemed only a little time until the five weeks were out. Al had qualified as an aerial gunner with a high score. His record had been so good that he might easily have applied for and been accepted as a gunnery instructor, but he had joined the Air Force to fight and he did not make his application. He was assigned to bomber training center and one day, with his orders in his pocket, he climbed on a train to go to the place where bomber crews are assembled and trained as a unit. And it seemed to him very long ago that he had mixed chocolate sodas and poured caramel syrup over dishes of ice cream for giggling girls. He didn't seem the same young man who had done these things, and the fact of the matter was that he was not the same young man. He had none of the great words of the newspapers and the propagandists on his tongue. Probably he could not have put into words the urge he felt, but it was an urge toward action. Like a hunter he wanted to see live game in his sight, and when his work was done he wanted to see the smoke of a destroyed enemy trailing behind a falling ship. He was the hunter of the air, the stinger in the tail of the long range bomber, and he wanted to join his group.

The hits are counted and stamped on an aerial target

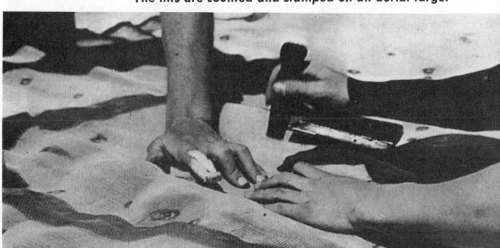

THE NAVIGATOR

THE purpose of a long-range bomber is to fly to a given target and to drop its bombs. That is the simple statement of it and its complication arises in the technique of getting the bomber to the target and getting it home again. The bombardier is there to drop the bombs on the target. The pilot will guide and control the ship. The crew chief will see to the engines. The gunner protects the plane from attack and the radio operator keeps up communication with ground and other planes. But bombers, given a pin point to go to, must have navigators to tell them how to get there. A plane cannot fly by sight over seas and deserts or at night or in clouds and arrive at its destination, any more than a ship can.

The aerial navigator is a very necessary member of a bomber crew. The word navigation, referring as it does to the sea, is misused, but apparently it is going to continue to be misused. An attempt was made to change aerial navigation to avigation with practically no success at all, for navigation seems to have lost its exclusive reference to the sea and will refer to any directed travel by instrument and map. Aerial navigation is not much different from marine navigation except that things happen more quickly. The basic instruments are the same, the compass to tell the direction in which you are going and the sextant and chronometer to tell you where you are. Other instruments—air-speed indicators, drift meters, etc.—are more recent inventions and their use is limited to airplanes. The basic instruments are very ancient. The compass has only changed in accuracy since early Chinese seamen placed a little lodestone bar on a chip of wood and floated the chip in a saucer.

The modern compass is a marvel of accuracy, but its principle is that of the lodestone on a chip—that a magnet will point toward magnetic North. Gioja's refinement in the fourteenth century was only followed by a long series of refinements and corrections, and the principle of crossed staff and astrolabe is carried through in the marvelously accurate modern sextant and octant.

The modern radio time signal is the completely accurate grandchild of the well-built and protected chronometer, and the aerial navigator is the child of the sea captain who shot sun and star from his quarter-deck and brought his ship over the curve of the earth to an unseen port. The aerial navigator, of all members of a bomber crew, except possibly the gunner, practices an ancient profession, and of all the members of the crew the navigator needs more technical education and training. The ideal candidate for commission as aerial navigator in the Army Air Force will have some background in mathematics and in astronomy. Engineers make good navigators because, in addition to the basic knowledge, they have acquired the method of thinking and studying which is required at Army Air Force Navigation Schools. Such engineering training, however, is not required.

The navigator enters the Army Air Force in the same way as do the bombardier and pilot. He makes application and is sent to an induction center where he is tested physically and mentally before he is assigned to Navigation School. The navigator candidate will have a different temperament from pilot and bombardier. He is rather more studious and more a perfectionist in his work. There is no "fairly close" in navigation. The point indicated must be found exactly. For example, a squadron of bombers rarely takes off from the same place. Individual planes may leave from different stations with orders to rendezvous at a given place and at a given time. In each plane it will be the navigator's job to get his ship to that place in the sky at a given moment. His work must be exact, else his ship will not be in its place in the flight.

When the navigation cadet has passed the physical and mental tests, the manual aptitude tests, and so forth, he will be assigned to a school. The school and the course will be described as follows. Its objective is to qualify students as navigator members of a combat crew. Its scope—qualification as precision, dead-reckoning, and celestial navigators and qualification as junior officer members of the combat crew. The duration of the course is fifteen weeks. The course is divided into two parts, flying training and ground school, and in this particular school there will be more ground work than flying work for the navigator has a great deal to learn.

In ground school he will learn dead-reckoning navigation. He will learn instruments, maps and charts, radio navigation. In celestial navigation he will learn the general theory, time and hour angle, instruments, star identification, and astronomical triangles. In meteorology he will learn the theory and principles of weather analysis, the interpretation of weather maps, the discussion of forecasts. He will learn the meteorology of the ocean, of thunderstorms, tornadoes, and icing conditions, and on top of all of it, as in every other Air Force school, he will have constant athletic and military training.

When he finishes the course he will be able to take a ship or a plane to any given point. During his school the work will be hard and constant, but if the student has the fortitude, the mind, and the body, and can take it, he will emerge from his school an essential part of the bomber team. In his hands will lie responsibility for direction, for knowing the winds and the drift, for knowing the earth and the currents of the air. On the navigator's direction, the pilot will find the enemy whether it be an invading ship near Midway Island, a submarine base in

Navigation classroom

the Aleutians, or a tank factory in Europe. When the target is found, his work will be over while bombardier releases his bombs, and then, again, the navigator must take the direction of the ship, must find the way home, must find the little point of land with the runways where the bomber will come to rest. The success of the bombing mission, a great part of it, is very definitely in the navigator's hands. He is an indispensable member of the bomber team.

Allan had got his degree in Civil Engineering and was two months in postgraduate work for an electrical engineering degree when the war broke out. His father was county engineer in a central Indiana county and had been for twenty years. Allan knew he was fit for the Army and would eventually be in the Army. He thought of applying for the Engineers Corps, but the Air Force seemed to him the more interesting Service. Like every other young man in the country, he thought he would like to be a pilot. That was natural enough. When uninstructed people thought of the Air Force, they used to think only of pilots. The great organization of ground crews and air crews rarely occurred to them. They have read only of pilots. The heroes in their magazine stories have been pilots. Newspapers have spoken almost exclusively of pilots, yet the pilot is actually only one part of the functioning Air Force.

It cannot be successfully argued that without the pilots the planes do not fly, for without any part of the Air Force the ships do not fly, without weather men and mechanics, without commanders and enlisted men. An error by a grease monkey will bring down a plane as surely as an error by a pilot. It is a force of split responsibility. No one position is more important than another. It is true that the pilot is most in evidence and has been treated most romantically in the press, but the pilot himself knows as well as any, and better than most, how much he must rely on the ground maintenance crew, on navigator and radio man. An Army pilot knows that he is not the fair-haired boy of the Air Force. There isn't any fair-haired boy. The force must function as a unit. One might as well say that the controls of a plane are more important and necessary than the engine or that the air foil is more important than the propellers. The plane does not take the air unless every part functions successfully and the Air Force does not function unless all of its men do their jobs. This is very well known in the Air Force. It is only civilians who think of the pilot as separate and more important and romantic than his brothers. But Allan had read the usual things and he, like many others, thought of the Air Force as a group of lordly officers who were pilots with valets to service their planes. He made application for training and was accepted on his scholastic record, for in engineering school he had a background of mathematics, a training in the use of instruments, several courses in astronomy, the controlled thinking that goes with mathematics and the discipline toward exactness that goes with engineering. His application was accepted and he was sent to an induction center and there his hair was clipped with all the others. He drew his work clothes and his neat khaki uniform. He was given the intelligence test and the aptitude test, the interviews and physical examinations, and finally Allan was called to a private interview with an officer. He stood nervously waiting for the unknown. The officer said quietly, "At ease, sit down there." He had a report on the desk in front of him. He glanced down at the papers and then up at Allan. "You have a good rating here," he said. "There is nothing in this report to indicate that you would not make a good pilot. Some difficulty might show up in training, but it isn't likely. Physical and mental reports are both good." Allan began to breathe again. "Thank you, sir," he said.

"There is something in this background and report I want to talk about," the officer went on. "You should be a good pilot, but with your engineering background you should make an even better navigator." Allan leaned forward in his chair. "I thought I'd like to be a pilot," he said. "Everyone wants to be a pilot," the officer said, "but we need navigators as much as we need pilots. The ships have to get to the targets and back. It isn't a second-choice job. On your record, I would like to recommend you for navigation school. After fifteen weeks, if you pass, you will be commissioned a second lieutenant. Your ground pay and your flying pay will be the same as a pilot and rank and promotion are on the same basis. And you must understand that a navigator is not a washed-out pilot. He is a specialist in his own line and your background qualifies you particularly. Think it over and report to me tomorrow morning."

Allan sat in the induction center post exchange, drinking cokes and thinking it over. His mind was quick to grasp implications. The specialty he was offered was work for all his life. He knew that when the war is over a great part of the commerce of the world will be air-borne, that great ships and possibly strings of towed gliders will carry the people and the produce of the world from place to place. He knew that, except for short hauls, the old methods of transportation, ships and rails and trucks, were going to disappear because they were slower and more expensive and less efficient than air transportation. In college he had talked often with students and instructors about the future of air commerce, and all of these ships would need navigators and the route plotters and dispatchers would be navigators. It was a whole life work that was being offered him, and it seemed to him a better and more interesting life than a civil engineering job which, during his memory at least, had been precarious.

He went to the counter and got another coke and sat down again. The war was going on. It had to be fought and won. If he wanted action, he would have it. A bomber doesn't hide its head, even its defensive work is attack. He would see all the action he wanted and would take a definite and important part in it and when the war was won, he had a profession which would continue to be action. Allan had always done his own thinking. He went over the question carefully. Pilots would be necessary too after the war, but there would be a great many more pilots than aerial navigators. There would be all the combat pilots and the copilots, all the thousands of civil pilots. Navigators would be very definitely in demand. In the middle of his third coke, he thought with some guilt how he was considering a future in peace and was selfishly figuring what he would gain. It was true, the future of the navigator, and it was to be considered. And now that he had considered it, he shut it out of his head. There was a war to be fought, and he was very tired of coke. As he walked back to his quarters he thought how he would see the world at war and would see it at peace, all of the world, the cities and peoples of the Orient and of South America. He would help to carry food to the new-born peoples of Europe when the German locust was killed and driven out. Probably the seed which would make Europe fruitful again would be carried through the air. If he wanted to see the life of his planet during his own time he could not want a better profession.

The next morning, after a second interview, he was assigned to an aerial navigation school.

Aerial navigation is a technical job. It is learned in the classroom and the laboratory, and for that matter the laboratory, the training plane AT-7, are classrooms themselves. In each ship there are three desks and three sets of instruments so that three students may work at the same time. Classrooms in the training centers look like any classrooms. They are long and the desks are arranged in line. At the front is the instructor's stand with a blackboard behind it, while on the instructor's table and on his stand are the demonstration equipment he uses as he lectures to his class. The room looks like other schoolrooms, but there its similarity stops. In the cadet classrooms are no sleepy students slopping in their seats, no whispering or writing of notes, no horseplay. There isn't time for it. The class marches to its desks. Each man stands at attention until he is ordered to be seated. He sits up at his desk with his eyes forward on the demonstrable assumption that an alert posture is concomitant of an alert mind.

In the navigation school a great deal must be learned in a

very short time. The work has been designed to be as much as a very good man can stand. A second-rate man cannot stand it at all, but with the initial testing a second-rate man rarely gets into navigation school.

Allan marched to his desk and stood stiffly until the class was ordered to be seated. The instructor did not waste any time. He went quickly into the definitions of navigation. On the sphere before him, which represented the earth's surface, he explained the system of co-ordinates, meridians and parallels, latitude and longitude. He explained the great circles and small circles, the difference between a great circle course and the mercator course. He spoke of the statute mile and the nautical mile. In the first classes the different projections of maps were discussed, the Lambert-Conformal Conic projection and the Mercator projection, gnomonic, stereographic, and other projections, and the methods of measuring course and distance on each. Definition was immediately followed by application in every case. And after each set of definitions there was a quick questioning of the class not only to find out how much the individuals had learned, but to set in their minds what they had learned.

But the navigation school was not solely class work. Their military drill and formation was as rigid and continuous as that of any other school in the Air Force; and from class they went to the athletic fields where they played the active games the Air Force encourages, football and basketball, volleyball and baseball, obstacle races, running and jumping. After the hours in the classroom they needed the playing fields to shake the kinks out of their backs. They hadn't really time to get tired and after the class work and the athletics were done and the formations were done and they had eaten their dinner, it was still a good idea to get out the textbooks and to study what had gone on during the day. For the work goes very rapidly and it is difficult to go back and pick up.

Navigation class practicing with the octant

The training ships for navigators are AT-7's, twin-engine, all-metal ships equipped really as flying classrooms in navigation. Along the right-hand side of the plane are three desks for three cadets and beside each desk is a drift meter and a compass. In back of the pilot, and in sight of all the desks, there is an auxiliary instrument board with dials showing altitude and air speed and air temperature—in fact, all the information that is needed for a navigator to do his work. In the roof of the ship there is a turret through which the navigator can shoot the sun or a star to find his position. The driftmeter is really a simple instrument: a glass, through which one can look down through the floor of the plane, on which are parallel lines. A knob al-

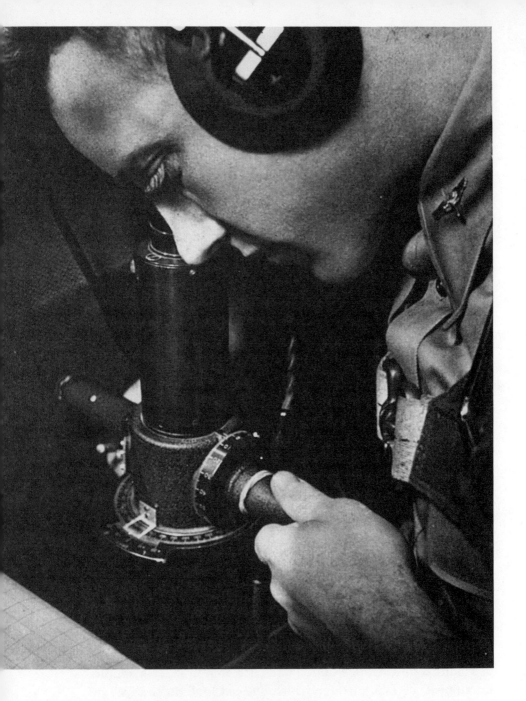

Navigation cadet looks through the driftmeter

lows one to rotate the field of the glass. Looking down through it the navigator finds an object on the ground, a tree or a house, and catches it in the parallel lines of the glass. Then, by rotating his glass, he makes the object stay within the parallel lines and not slide across them. Having done this, a relation is established in the figures on the side of his instrument which gives him the amount of his side drift. At night he drops a flare to use as an object.

In these flying classrooms each student plots the course, takes position, each without consulting the other. It is in this way that immediate application of the lessons of the classroom is obtained.

In the beginning the cadets use their octants outside the classroom until they become familiar with the use of the instrument. In the classroom Allan learned the use of the plotting sheet. He prepared plans for flights he would later fly, by plotting in the locations of airports, lighthouses, and other actual objects in the immediate area. He learned map symbols and how to do pilotage.

The class studied the magnetic compass and its variations and deviations. The other instruments used by the navigator were studied, altimeters and air-speed meters, air-temperature thermometers, the airplane clock, directional gyro, the artificial horizon, bank and turn indicators, rate-of-climb indicators, and automatic pilots. Study and practice were constant and simultaneous. They studied the celestial sphere and practiced in identifying stars, estimating their declination and hour angle. They learned the names of constellations and of the navigational stars. They committed to memory the pattern of each constellation and the names of the navigational stars in each constellation, and finally all of the accumulated knowledge was put into the practice navigation plan. Here was the study of the mission to be accomplished, the rate and alternate routes, the weather forecasts for the area, and emergency landing fields along the route were chosen, each student for himself.

The physical aids to navigation were filled in the plan, radio stations, light beacons, prominent landmarks. The plan for observation was included, data on celestial bodies to be observed. The navigation plan considered all circumstances and all accidents and deviations so that the mission would surely be carried out.

Throughout all the work the mission is of first importance. Now all the apparently unrelated lessons began to fall into place. Of the whole bomber crew the work of the navigator is the most intellectual. He does not handle any control of the plane. His work is committed to paper. He makes a map of what the ship will do and where it will go, and when his map is made he guides the ship through his figures to its objective and home again.

The ship is a pin point hovering over a globe with sun and stars swinging over it and the navigator must know every moment exactly where he is in relation to all space. Allan's class moved through its course, working and studying too hard even to know they were working hard. Armed with their figures and their facts and their instruments they made practice flights and were a little surprised to find that the formulae worked, that the ship went to the spot on the earth which was the spot on the map. Navigation is good clean work and there is a great satisfaction in plotting the course of a flight and carrying it out.

Someone once described navigation as being broken up into three phases—(1) determining a place to go; (2) determining how to get there, and (3) determining that you get there. Navigation is work for a perfectionist. It is not enough to come close to a given spot. A closeness is as worthless as a great miss. Three planes take off at different times and at night. Their mission is to meet at a spot over the world which is not marked and to

Practical navigation in flight

meet in the dark at a given moment. The basic instruments are stars and time to which man-made instruments are applied by the prime instrument of all, the navigator. If he misses his unmarked place by even a mile or gets there inaccurately in point of time, the rendezvous will not be made.

Navigators should be able to navigate by dead reckoning means with a maximum course error of one degree and maximum E.T.A. (estimated time of arrival) error of 1½ minutes per hour of flight since the last landmark or fix. They must be able to navigate during daylight by celestial means to within 25 miles of objective over distances approximating the full tactical range of aircraft; while during darkness they must be able

Through the top turret of the training plane a navigation cadet takes a night shot with his octant

to navigate by celestial means to within 15 miles of objective over distances approximating full tactical range of aircraft. And finally they must be able to locate reasonable objectives at night under blackout conditions from a definite landpoint 25 to 50 miles away from the objective with pilot taking evasive action.

Allan's class made its maps and its flight plans. Allan was becoming a navigator. He felt the pleasure of directing the ship by his observation. Every day there was a new mission, its object to put to use the recently learned lesson. They flew in all weather, day and night. The weeks went on and the graduation flight came into preparation.

This is numbered Mission 20. It is a long celestial flight and is described as follows: "This mission will be the graduation flight and consists of three flights of at least four hours' duration. This mission should simulate a tactical mission to complete the transition necessary for the student to apply all the technique he has learned to the tactical navigational requirements. It should be in daylight and in darkness, the daylight portion to be over water. All methods of navigation will be practiced." It was a tactical mission, but it was much more than that. They would be navigators when they came back from it. The flight plans were made several days in advance. No two ships were taking quite the same course, yet all of them would fly the legs of a huge triangle and the two points away from camp were near cities. Further it was rumored that the cadets would be entertained at the two stops. For fourteen weeks the class had not rested. They had hardened on drill ground and athletic field. Civilian flesh had melted away and its place was taken by harder flesh, disciplined flesh. The cadet did not get so tired now, but sleep was still the most desirable thing in the world. There never was enough of that.

They drew up the flight plans for Mission 20 with great care and all of the class shaved extra close and had new haircuts for the flight. They checked their sextants for error and went over their little cases of instruments. The silver ships were warming up on the line. The navigation cadets drew their parachutes and lounged in the squadron room waiting for their time, and then they lined up and the squadron leader spoke to them shortly. The formation marched out to the line where the engines of the AT-7's were idling now. They broke up and three cadets went to each plane. Each one sat at a little desk and adjusted his head set and plugged in on the communication system. They laid out their maps on the desks and studied them. The metal doors slammed shut. The ships moved out one by one to the runway. The pilot looked back at the three cadets bent over their desks. He smiled for a moment. He picked up his microphone and his voice was in the ears of his students. "Here we go," he said, and he switched the speaker to the tower. Safety belts were fastened, parachutes buckled over legs, and the shoulder harness over the seat backs where it could easily be reached.

From the tower the take-off instructions blasted in their ears. "Roger," the pilot said and put his two throttles ahead.

It was afternoon when the flight started. The silver ships leaped up into the air one after another and circled once for altitude. Allan could see the fields below with the lines of barracks, with the parade ground and the columns of young men drilling. The work had been so hard that he had not seen it in the whole before, but now this phase of his training was over and at each of the stops they would be met by local people. They would go to dances and be fed, and when they came back they would be commissioned and assigned.

Through his window, Allan could see another plane shimmering in the sun beside him. He had not had time to think in the top of his mind about anything but navigation. His eye went to the altimeter, 3,000 feet. He wondered where he would be assigned as an instructor; his grades had been good but he didn't want to be an instructor. Perhaps he would navigate one of the big transports with food and supplies to the fighting world, but there were older men who could do that. No, he hoped he would go out on one of the big ships with a belly full of bombs. He hoped an electric plant or a factory would rise in a red roar because of his navigation. Or best of all he hoped he might find an invasion fleet as the big ships did at Midway and help to strew the ocean with the hopes of conquerors. That was the best of all. But mostly he hoped to be on a fighting ship that carried bombs. He looked at his compass and then up at the altimeter again. The needle slid to 5,000 feet. He picked his mike from the clamp on the wall and pressed the button and he spoke the course into the pilot's ears. The pilot nodded. "Wilco," he said. The ship banked and leveled out again. Alan looked down at his compass. The ship was on his course.

Last minute instructions before a night cross-country flight

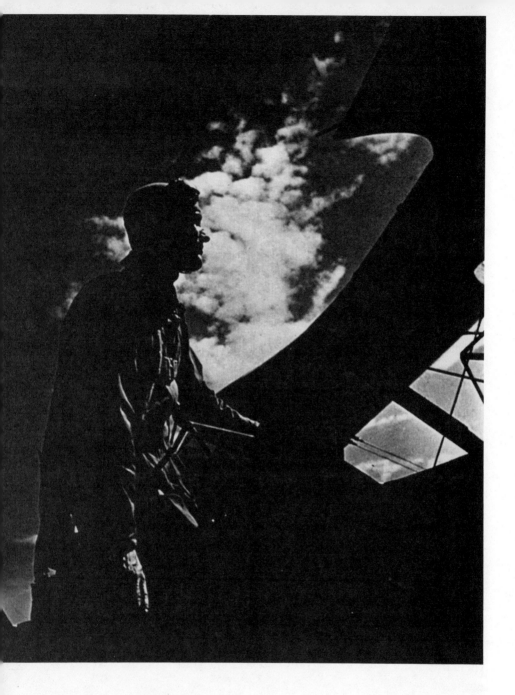

Cadet starts his training to be a pilot

THE PILOT

THE pilot is still in the public mind the darling of the Air Force. To the Air Force, however, he is only one of a number of specialists highly trained to carry out a military mission. But the public, led on by fiction and newspapers, still considers the pilot the overshadowing officer in an airplane. The reason for this is not far to seek. In early airplanes the pilot was all alone and, more, in the experimental period of heavier-than-air craft, the pilot was usually the man who had built and powered the plane he flew. Further, he was the only man in the world who knew the tricks of his ship well enough to fly it. A pilot did not change planes then. When one was crashed, he built another one. During the last war the airplane was used almost exclusively as an observation instrument. The ship flying over enemy lines came back and reported positions of enemy troops and artillery. But as soon as a ship went over your lines, you sent up ships to intercept him. And thus both ships came to be armed. Out of these observation missions, and their repulse, grew the romantic and courageous dogfights of the last war when individual pilots carried insignia and gained reputations like medieval knights. Then it became simply a matter of individual shooting down individual plane. Then names like Richthofen and Rickenbacker became the symbols of everything young men wanted to be. Later in the war, group flights to protect the observation planes were undertaken. And still there were the dogfights, but a new member had been added—the observer. While the ships were fighting, his job was to take photographs of enemy positions.

Single-seater planes had learned to fly low by then, spraying ground troops with their machine guns, and camouflage had developed to conceal guns and supplies. It was only toward the end of the war that the bomber came to be used and it was an inaccurate arm which actually threw high-explosive rocks at an enemy; and bombing did not develop colorfully enough to overshadow in the public mind those silver knights who met in single combat over the line while men looked on and cheered the victor and buried with full honors the vanquished, whether he was friend or enemy, and set his propeller over his grave. It was the ultimate in romantic combat, complete with trappings and roaring steeds and audience. Missions were fairly lax then and it was more important to have the marks of dead enemies on your ship than to have taken fine photographs. At least this was so with the public. The pilot was the king.

It was after the war that the complicated tactics of air warfare were developed. Then the mission became more important than the game. Then air forces became integrated groups waging warfare of attacks on ground objectives. Then fighter and pursuit ships became supplemental to the bomber. The bomber did the damage. It was the striking weapon. Pursuits and interceptors then were assigned to protect their own bombers and to attack the bombers of the enemy.

The development of the bomber required the addition of new kinds of air fighters; gunners, to protect the mission; bombardiers, to drop explosives accurately on a target; navigators, unerringly to find the target. And the targets changed too. Whereas the first bombs were aimed only at munitions dumps and troop concentrations and roads, the new targets were more profoundly far-reaching. The bombs sought the factories where munitions were made, the dynamos which created the power to run the plants, the rail lines and highways over which the tools of war were transported. Douhet wrote and Goering and Mussolini believed that if enough bombs were dropped on a civil

112

A cadet receives instruction about the design and construction of airplanes

population, nerves would break and the will to resist would disappear. It may be that this is true. It has been tried in Spain, in Poland, and in England and it has not succeeded yet, but that may be because not enough bombs were dropped. Ten times the number might have done the job. The number dropped so far have only succeeded in making peoples angry and resistant and vengeful. What does work, however, is the destruction of plants, shipyards, docks, ships, and transportation systems, and these have become the new targets for the bombers, just as the bomb-

113

ers have become the main weapons of the Air Force. With the development of the importance of the bomber, the pilot too has changed his status. He is no longer individually the most important man in the Air Force. Just as the ship is a highly complicated unit, so the air crew is considered as a unit, each member of which is equally important. The newspapers still to a certain extent dwell lovingly on the pilot, but the Air Force itself knows that the eye at the bombsight and the finger on the trigger of the blister guns are equally important. This does not mean that individual heroism is finished. On the contrary, it has increased, but a pilot can no longer go to death and glory alone. His crew and his mission put brakes on his knight errantry, and to the pursuit pilot the mission is of more importance than the shooting down of enemies too. Indeed, in England the refusal of the Royal Air Force to rise up in single combat, although they were taunted and reviled, was probably the saving, not only of their Air Force, but of England too. For, by refusing to fight individually, they later were able to drive the German bombers out of the English skies.

Air Force tactics have definitely become group tactics where men and machines work together toward an objective. And under this system the pilot has changed his status. He is only one part of the functioning unit, but far from making him less highly trained, he has become more so. It is more difficult to fly as one ship in a formation than as one ship in the sky.

The training of a bomber pilot is a long and difficult matter. He must know a great deal and he must be perfectly fitted for his job, but he is no longer the apex of the Air Force pyramid. After he has mastered his machines the pilot will be constantly trained in teamwork. He must have initiative, but it must be subordinated to and used for the group; and it is this ability of Americans, exemplified in their team sports of being both individuals and units in a group at the same time, which makes them

114

A man in the control tower directs the primary planes with a red and green light

both the finest team players and the finest flyers in the world. Each quality alone would be ineffective—together they are unbeatable. It might have been thought that the relaxing of the college requirement for pilot cadets would result in a lower standard among pilots. But this has not been true, either in effect, nor in intention. It was realized that some of our brightest, best-informed boys have not gone to college. They have studied at home, have taken correspondence courses, or have read and tinkered extensively. It is not possible for all of our young people capable of college training to go to college. The removal of the college requirement by the Air Force, by removing an artificial hurdle, tapped a large group of Americans who were not able to go to college but who kept up anyway. The quality of mind and body is not changed. The examinations are not relaxed. They eliminate the college man as well as the noncollege man if he is unfit for the Service, and we have too many eminent examples of noncollege men to overlook this rich pool of potential flyers. The alert, strong, the well-co-ordinated and interested young men of the country are the proper candidates for pilots. The work they do will test deeply every part of them. They will emerge from their wartime service with an honorable record and a profession. They will have seen action where there is any action. The wings they wear will make them for all time a part of the brotherhood of the air. They will have space and speed in the palms of their hands but they must deliver the goods if these things are to be theirs.

In the Air Force you must deliver the goods from the moment you enter. Step by step, you must deliver the goods and there is no second chance, a man is only washed out when he cannot perform. It would be ridiculous for him to have another chance for it is not a matter of chance. From the moment he enters his first primary training plane to the time when he graduates from four-motor school, the training pilot works like a dog. But he comes out a magnificent pilot. At any point he may have failed. If he finishes, he is as good a pilot as it is possible to produce. Muscles and nerves and discipline will be hard. He will know ships and men. He will be a flying officer in the Army Air Force and that's as good a man as you can be in any army.

The ship will be in his finger tips and in his knowledge. As with the other members of a bomber crew, the Air Force has the pick of the country. It selects only the best in mind and body, and in spite of the growing need of our sky-rocketing Air Force the country can produce the material. The young man wishing to be a pilot makes his application just as bombardier and navigator have and if he is accepted, on his past record, he goes to

the induction center just as they do. There he is put through the same tests. Perhaps he wanted to be a pilot and he is told that he will be a better bombardier, or perhaps the tests have shown that he has the qualifications for a pilot; but he will have been tested to his limit and the officers who recommend his branch will know all about him from the records they have made in the tests. If he has shown qualifications as a pilot he will become immediately an aviation cadet, and he will be assigned to a primary school to get his first training in flying an airplane.

Joe was a big, slow-talking boy from South Carolina. He was a farmer by birth and by tradition. He came out of the university knowing more about scientific farming than his father did

117

and more than his father would admit. Joe's two younger brothers were pretty confused because their father told them one thing and then Joe took them aside and told them another. Joe had his head full of phosphates and blooded cattle and things were shaping up for a fight on the farm, for Joe's father was a strong-willed man. And then the war came along and solved everything. Joe decided to let fertilizers and Holsteins go until the war was over.

He applied for entrance into the Air Force, and when he was accepted he left a pile of text books for his father; and the old man read them and got pretty excited about them once it wasn't a simple matter of disobedience on Joe's part. Joe was hardly off the place before his father bought a fine Holstein heifer. One of the young brothers wrote to Joe about it and told him not to mention it.

Meanwhile, at the induction center, Joe went through his tests and his interviews and it was discovered that his big, unhurried hand and his slow speech were by no means indications of a slow mind. When his tests were finished he was ticketed a cadet pilot and sent to one of the many civilian schools which, under Army control, give pilots their primary training. Class and drill and life was all Army but the instructors were civilians and the field was a civilian field. Perhaps this may not always be—perhaps, for that matter, by the time this is printed it will not be; but in the time when the Air Force must expand with almost explosive speed, every facility for training must be used. Civilian instructors are available and they undertake the first flying training of the cadet.

Joe landed in the camp and was assigned to his barracks and he was assigned to his instructor, a moth-eaten flying man who had barnstormed crates and raced for small purses and learned to fly by flying for twenty years. The name of Joe's instructor was Wilmer and he had a crooked leg and a broken nose. Wil-

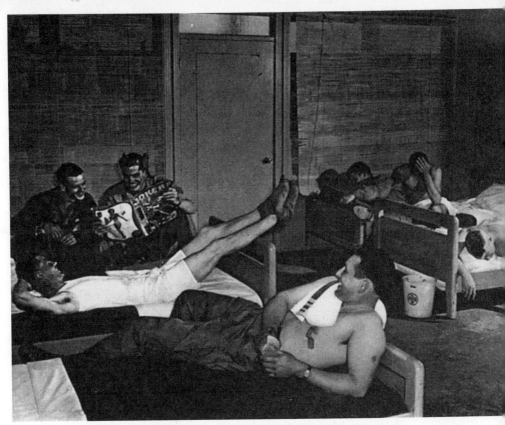

Primary cadets in their barracks after a hard day's flying

mer didn't waste any time. He took the students to the small primary trainers standing on the line and they walked around the little ship. Wilmer explained the rudder, the elevators, the ailerons, the principle of air foil. They leaned into the plane and he showed them the instruments, the controls, the throttle. He showed them how to start and stop the engine and then he turned to Joe and said, "Get in that rear seat and plug in the speaking tube."

It was that quick. Wilmer got into the forward seat and he showed Joe how to cinch his safety belt. "Now take the stick lightly in your hand and never jerk it. Work it around and get the feel of it. It will feel different in the air with an air flow

119

against it." Joe moved the stick forward and back and sideways. The elevators moved up and down when he pushed it up and back and the ailerons moved one up and one down when he waggled the stick sideways. Wilmer said "Now put your feet on the rudder. Don't kick it around, it is a gentle movement and it all works together. "Ever ride a horse?" "Sure," said Joe. "Ever ride a polo pony?" "In school." "Well," said Wilmer, "I'll tell you. Your feet on the rudder and your hand on the stick is almost exactly the same as reins and stirrups on a horse. Pull back on the reins or the stick and her head will come up. Push forward and she will take her head and bolt. When you make a turn you'll use both reins and stirrups. But don't do anything jerky any more than you would to a horse. Okay, let's go," Wilmer said. "You just hold on lightly and feel what I do."

He climbed in, speeded the motor, and moved out for the take-off. "Watch the tower," he said. "Get into the habit of watching the tower." He waggled his ailerons. Joe, watching the tower, saw a green light come on—the permission to take off.

The little motor roared. Joe's hand was on the throttle and the throttle went full ahead. Never again in his life could Joe, or anyone for that matter, know the breathless excitement of the first take-off with the controls in his hands and feet. True, Wilmer was doing it actively wth his controls, but Joe's hands felt every impulse in the dual control.

The little ship took off at fifty miles an hour, but it seemed to bolt over the ground. Joe felt the stick go gently forward, felt the tail rise, then the stick came evenly back a little and the weight on the wheels lightened. The plane bumped twice and took the air. Then the stick moved a little forward to level off for speed and then gently back again for altitude. A puff of wind wobbled them and Joe felt in the rudder and stick how Wilmer corrected for it. Then stick and rudder moved softly to the left and the ship turned and the controls came back to

After a dual flight period the instructor explains various maneuvers to the cadet

neutral and the turn continued. A little stick and rudder to the right and the ship straightened out and the stick came back a little and they climbed. There is nothing like the first flight. It can never be repeated and the feeling of it can never be duplicated. It is a new dimension discovered, but discovered in the nerve ends and in the exploring ganglia of the brain, and no amount of flying in passenger ships can do it. The little plane balanced on air, tippy as a canoe and as dependable in the hands of a flyer, and the whole floating like a leaf and responsive to the lightest touch, and the feeling is flight and pride and a strange sense of power and freedom.

The great law has been broken. Probably men have wanted

121

to revolt against the law of gravity since they first noticed that birds and some insects are given a dispensation against it. The great envy that children have of birds, the dreams of flying if one only knew a trick with the hands or could press a magic button under the arm, the complete hunger for flight that is in all of us—all these are answered in the first take-off. Later the preoccupation will be with methods and techniques and instruments, but the first pure joy in release, there is nothing like it. These things, these thoughts and words, have been trite until it happens to you and then the feeling is ringed with fire.

The noise was loud in the plane. Wilmer pointed a finger at the altimeter dial. The needle was at 3,700 feet and rising. When it came to 4,000 the stick went a little forward and Wilmer's voice came to Joe through the rubber ear pieces. "Straight and level flight. Pull back the throttle. Now, look at the horizon, hold it there." And Joe saw that the plane was in his hands, the instructor was not touching the controls. He felt something like a bubble swell in his chest. "We're going to make a left turn," Wilmer said. "Now, stick and rudder together." The left wing rode gently down and from his left window Joe could see the earth beneath. "That's enough—stick and rudder back to neutral."

The plane flew in a great circle. "Now straighten her out. Don't strangle the stick." Joe moved stick and rudder to the right. The plane straightened and he neutralized his controls and suddenly he knew he had done it all himself, without help. "Watch your ailerons," Wilmer said. "See they're lined up with the wings. Now, right turn. That's enough. Straighten out. You were jerky on that one. Try a left turn. That was better. Urge it, don't push it." So they went, right, left, straight and level, climbing turns, descending turns, no time to waste. You can only learn to fly by flying. Gentle and medium turns, and finally Wilmer said, "All right, let's go back. There is the tower,

122

cut your throttle. Now, hold her nose up. She wants to put it down." Joe felt the weight of the nose on the stick and he held back against it. He followed Wilmer's hands while they landed that first day, felt him come in and then pull back to drop the tail, and they taxied to the line. Joe loosened his belt and climbed stiffly out. He was wet with perspiration. Wilmer grinned at him, "You'll be all right. You'll have to relax, but that'll come." Another cadet walked up and Wilmer said, "All right, get in the rear seat and fasten your safety belt."

Joe watched the take-off. It was a slow plane. There was nothing so wonderful about it. And then he remembered what it had been like, the most wonderful thing in the world, sensitive and gentle, every wind and every air current it touched, moved it. It moved like a canoe. He shivered, something had happened to him that would never go away. A new element was opened and he had stepped into it and he would never be a groundling again.

It is a strange, almost mystical thing that happens to flying men. It is as though the experience had cut them off so that they can only communicate with their own kind, can only be understood by other flying men. When they meet they go away together and perhaps they don't talk about flying, although that isn't likely. But at least they know and understand each other. They have been through something that has the impact of religion, and while most of them are never able to say it, never want to say it, they all understand it. And in his first day Joe had his first glimpse into the inside of this brotherhood. There is another thing that flyers have in common with good sailors— they never lose respect for the ship. They never take it lightly, never know it well enough to hold it in contempt. A man cannot fly without a ship and a ship cannot fly without a man. Perhaps it is his participation which gives him his strong feeling about airplanes, and once a man has entered the brotherhood it

123

With a model plane the instructor demonstrates maneuvers to his students

is a rare thing for him to leave it. A flying man remains a flying man until some force outside himself drags him down from the sky. Age or failing eyes or bad nerves may bring him down, but a man is never grounded by himself. His association with the new dimension is permanent.

Joe started in the air right away, but he started ground school too. As everywhere in the Air Force there was so much to learn, so quickly. In class they studied chemical warfare, the principal gases and why each was used, and they learned to recognize each kind and the protection against each kind. They learned to use gas masks and how to give first aid to a man overcome with gas. Next the class studied the planes of our Allies and

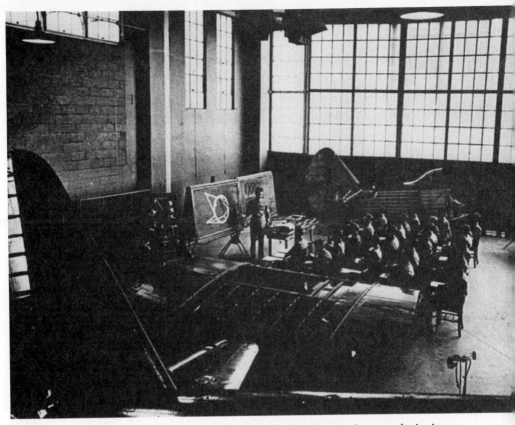

Ground school class in engines and airplanes

our enemies. It is very necessary to recognize a ship quickly and at a distance. And so with models and silhouettes they learned to recognize British and American and German and Japanese aircraft. With the models they learned to recognize the principal types at all angles. After instruction they had range estimation. A model was held up quickly and then concealed while the class wrote down nationality and type. They learned the capacities of different ships, how fast they could fly, how they maneuvered, what the fire power was, where they were well armored, and what were their weak and blind places. They learned to recognize a ship instantly. Next the class studied navigation. For in a single-place ship, in interceptors and fight-

125

ers, the pilot can carry no navigators. They studied the air-speed meter and the altimeter, the magnetic compass with its errors, variations, and deviations. They studied maps in different projection, learned to read maps, to measure courses and distances; vector problems were introduced and triangle of velocity problems. Dead-reckoning navigation was introduced, time, speed, and distance relations and the keeping of the simple log.

Meanwhile, every day they were in the air. With his instructor in the forward seat, Joe practiced "S" turns across roads. The instructor stalled the motor and taught him how to pull out of spins and stalls. Joe practiced take-offs and landing and now the instructor did not touch the controls. Joe did it all, but the voice of Wilmer was in his ears all the time, correcting him and informing, "You were jerky there, take it slowly. A little more rudder and a little less stick. You overstick some. Bring her in now. I think you're a little high, you'll overshoot. Let her go up and come in again." And hour by hour Joe's hand grew lighter on the stick and his feel for the rudder more delicate. The ship was getting into his system and he had confidence in his hands.

That is, he had confidence until his first solo. That was a lonely thing. He felt it before he got the green light from the tower. Wilmer was standing beside the runway watching him. Joe perspired a little. The light showed and he pushed the throttle forward. There was no voice in his ear now. He pushed his stick forward a little soon and that made him nervous and then he pulled it back and he rose too sharply, knew he was doing it. He had the stage fright of a young dancer, making little errors before an expert. And he could feel the instructor's eyes on him.

When he got altitude he calmed down a little and went through the turns and climbs and "S's" prescribed. He seemed jerky to himself. His faults glared in his own mind, too much stick there and on the next turn, too much rudder, overcompensating. He looked out and saw his ailerons off center and blushed and corrected them. Now his time was up and he made his approach for a landing. Too high, he usually was, well this time he wouldn't be. He came in too low and too fast, slowed and dropped in too fast. His hand was shaking now, not with fright, but because he knew the instructor was seeing everything. He dropped in, bounced and ballooned a little, and finally came to a stop. It was the worst landing he had ever made, even the first time he had brought it in.

Joe was hot all over. He wondered whether he would be washed out on the strength of a performance like that. He hated to turn and taxi back to face the man who had instructed him, but he did. Wilmer stood beside the ship, his face inscrutable. "That was awful," Joe said weakly. "Pretty bad," said Wilmer. "That balloon." "You're nervous," Wilmer told him. "That wasn't a good performance but it wasn't a terribly bad first solo. Did the balloon scare you?" "It made me mad," said Joe. "Look," Wilmer said, "it isn't good to sleep on a thing like that. Go up again, make one circle and come in."

The green light showed again. This time the tail came up evenly. Joe pulled off the ground and leveled for speed and climbed. At 700 feet he turned and came around and made his approach again and his hand didn't shake this time. The instructor had recognized pure stage fright. Joe came down and leveled off. Perhaps it was luck this time. His wheels grazed the ground and settled gently and his hand soothed the tail down. Joe felt wonderful. He loved Wilmer and he loved the ship. It was a perfect landing. He came about and taxied back to the line. Wilmer looked in at him. "That was a little bit better," Wilmer said. "I think you were a little high on that approach." Joe walked humbly off the field. There is something very humbling about an airplane. Now and then an H P, a hot

127

First solo flight

pilot, one who is cocky, develops, but not very often. The ships keep pilots humble, the best pilots that is.

Joe sat down on a bench for a moment. He held up his right hand and looked at it. The fingers were still shivering a little. He looked back at the line. Another cadet was in the ship. Joe watched the take-off. The tail came up too late and the take-off was too steep. Joe felt critical. "Too steep," he said to himself and then he laughed at himself. The second supervised solo and the third did not cause the emotional tumult of the first day. Joe's confidence was high now.

The instructors are curious men, for while they work with mechanics and flight they work also with very malleable human material. They must be excellent practicing psychologists, knowing when a word of praise makes the difference of a week in training and when a good bawling out will prevent a future accident.

A man's soul is pretty much in his instructor's hand during the first days. The instructor learns instinctively when a man is frightened and how to overcome that. He can feel nervousness in his dual stick. He can feel it in the wobble of the ship and by his knowledge of men he can make the student relax, can give him confidence without cockiness. Good instructors wash out fewer men than bad ones. They are almost uniformly stern men with acid tongues when they want to use them. They know their students at a glance, and they are as important to the student pilot's whole future as the first teacher in school is to a boy's whole education. And although they are well paid and their work is vital, nearly all the instructors would much rather be flying bombers into action. They complain constantly. "If I were only ten years younger, I'd have a B-17E right over Burma now."

Every day Joe went up and he was graded every day on his take-offs and landings and his action in the face of field traffic. In the fourth week he began his spot landing, which is rather like pitching pennies at a mark only harder. Judgment of speed and height and distance become more and more exact. The ships used a 90-degree approach from 500 feet and landed for a designated spot. And now Wilmer went up with him again and taught him elementary 8's, curves, and the climbing turn which is called a chandelle and which is practiced so much that elementary schools are called chandelle colleges. And finally the spot landings were graded by the instructor.

The work on the Link trainer began in the fourth week. This is a small mechanical model of a ship, just large enough to hold a man. It has the instruments of a ship and the controls. It can

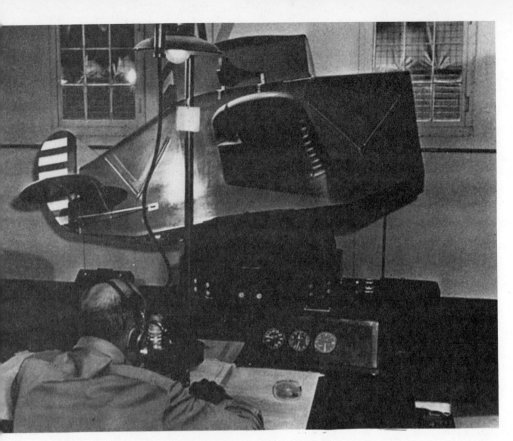

The cadet learns instrument flying inside a Link Trainer

make all the movements of a plane too, although it is only on a pivot. And apart from the Link trainer and yet controlled by it, an inked wheel describes on a chart exactly what the ship is doing. A trainer will spin and slip and it can be pulled out by its own controls. Furthermore, the instructor, sitting apart at his controls, can create nearly all the conditions that a ship may meet—heavy weather, rising and falling currents, head winds, side winds. With the cover down, a student can learn instrument flying on the Link trainer and the course he flies will be indicated by the inked line on the chart in front of the instructor. A great deal of flying experience can be had in a short time in a Link trainer and so successful has it proved itself that commissioned pilots are required to use it constantly to keep in practice. Beginning instrument flying is always taught in the trainer.

In the sixth week, there was practice at forced landings. Wilmer went up with Joe and directed him to a place over power lines, fences, and orchards, and then suddenly cut the engine. Then it was Joe's problem to pick out a place to land and by turning and gliding to approach it and to come down for a landing. But just before the wheels touched the instructor turned on the motor again and they went up and looked for another difficult place and did it all over. This training develops judgment of distance and surfaces and it also provides the basis for saving a pilot's life if he is in trouble.

In the seventh week there was dual and solo practice in 180-degree overhead approaches, lazy 8's and pylon 8's, and chandelles. There was advanced acrobatics, snap rolls, slow rolls, and Immelmann turns. In this week, Joe began his night flying.

In the classroom the cadets studied weather, its importance to flying. They learned weather services and the organization of airplane teletype report. They studied ceiling, cloudiness, and visibility as they apply to flying, rain, snow, sleet, and drizzle, fog, smoke, and haze, winds and wind shifts. They learned to read and make weather charts. This was the work with and about planes, but at the same time they were soldiers. Like all the other cadets they had their military drill daily and their athletics to keep them fit. Like all the other cadets during their training there was very little time to themselves. A letter written home now and then, a few moments in the post exchange to drink a coca-cola. In the barracks they talked flying, nothing but flying.

Recently a survey was made to find out what the cadets read and the answer is very simple. They don't read anything except their textbooks during their training. In the classrooms the

131

The cadet is taught slowrolls and other acrobatic maneuvers

study of airplanes themselves was undertaken, with models and parts; the study went on of parts, actions, and workings of planes. They studied air flow and pressure distribution on the wings, lift and induced drag and equilibrium in flight. With models and drawings the class learned what the invisible medium of the air does to ships in flight, where the pressures are and how they are utilized in flight, the aerodynamic effect of controls and flaps, the principles of the propeller of both fixed and variable pitch. They learned how a propeller can bite deep or shallowly into the air. Then again with models and parts they saw how a ship is built, how the wings are braced, and how strength and lightness are achieved. And when they had covered the ships they studied engines, four-stroke cycle engines and Diesel engines, and they learned the various engines used by the Air Force; air-cooled and liquid-cooled engines, the arrangement and functions of units; ignition systems and generators were torn down for explanation and there were working models to demonstrate mechanics. They studied fuels and lubricants and what kinds are used and why, fuel systems and carburetor systems, superchargers. They studied the instruments which check on engine action and signal any distress in any part. The class learned to operate various types of engines, to start and stop them, and finally they learned maintenance and repair and inspection and inspection symbols. From front to back they went over the ships until they knew the cable lines of the controls, the bracing structure, and the hydraulic pistons. It was a beginning study of how an airplane works, every part of it, why each part is built as it is and what its reaction to the air is.

This was the elementary flying school, and when they finished each student had sixty hours in the air—twenty-nine hours with an instructor and thirty-one hours of solo flying. They had flown by instruments and they had flown at night and each cadet had learned to navigate his plane and learned the traffic rules which are standard everywhere. They had been nine weeks at the school and in that time they had begun to be real flyers. At least they felt like pilots and probably they were the only men in the Air Force who thought they were. They talked flying and dreamed flying. Actually their work was only starting, they were just out of kindergarten. From primary school they would go to basic school, there to have many more hours in the air and much more theory.

In basic school they would learn about radio communications and how to prepare field messages and they would learn to use the radios in planes. Their study of the weather would be world-wide and they would learn methods of weather forecast from data. All of the study would be related to flying. Clouds would be taken up and how clouds indicate weather and what forecasts can be made from clouds. There was little time and much to learn.

Joe studied thunderstorms and hurricanes and their effect on flying. In basic school the old enemy, ice, was studied, the hazard of ice formations on the wings that have pulled down many ships. They learned the use of de-icers, the inflatable rubber wing and tail edges which crack the ice off and drop it away. Basic training was an enlargement of primary training. In flight Joe made turns and climbs, glides, stalls, spins, spirals, 8's, landings, and take-offs and forced landings, but now accuracy was demanded of him. He must be sure of his control of his ship. His spot landings must be perfect.

In his basic school there was a great emphasis on instrument flying. Nearly three hours every week were devoted to flying by instruments alone. For this training advanced-type Army ships were used, faster and more powerful ships. At the end of nine weeks at basic school, Joe had seventy more hours of flying and fifteen hours on the Link trainer. He had learned to fly a ship in formation with other ships, had learned the signals of forma-

Cadets in Advanced School go to their training planes, the At–9

tion so that he could space his ship perfectly with the others. And during the last week at basic school he had had transition flying in an advanced trainer. The nine weeks were over and this was the grammar school of the air. Advanced school followed and now Joe felt less a flyer than he had after his first solo. He had begun to see the actual complication of flying well and how much must be learned.

In elementary and basic school, airplanes alone had been the preoccupation, the flying of ships accurately from one place to another, keeping them out of trouble and maneuvering them. In advanced school the purpose of the military airplane began to emerge—attack and defense. Now, Joe studied not ships but military ships. Armament and attack became the main study. The history of pursuit aviation. The class studied Japanese and German pursuit and bombardment methods and their texts were the confidential reports on enemy ships in action. They studied the fighting techniques of the enemy and the methods of overcoming them and they learned our methods of attack, patrols, area protection, and strafing methods. Joe worked on pursuit formation and flight and squadron tactics. Night-fighting tactics were included with night landing systems, navigation at night, and methods of spotting enemy planes, barrage balloon and anti-aircraft guns. He learned about bombardment formation and tactical fire.

In advanced school, cadets suddenly stopped being simply pilots and became fighting pilots. In addition to being a pilot Joe had to be a gunner too. In advanced school there was a gunnery course. He learned the care and stripping of machine guns, both the .30- and the .50-caliber. In pursuit, the pilot is gunner too. Joe studied gunnery much as a gunnery school taught it. He fired at moving targets and learned the laws of lead and distance.

And now the class took up photograph interpretation and they learned the importance of rapid and accurate target identification and how to read aerial photographs. There came a new course in identification, the recognition of different types of naval units, again with models and silhouettes. Joe learned to identify battleships and battle cruisers, aircraft carriers, heavy cruisers, light cruisers, destroyers, and submarines. He learned enemy craft and our own and those of our Allies.

At the end of his advanced school Joe and his class were commissioned. They were no longer cadets but lieutenants. The bars were on their shoulders now and the silver wings on their left breasts. The cap ornaments were changed from propeller and wings to the eagles of officers, but they were still students. Joe

The instructor is ready to take the cadet on his first flight in an At–9

changed his living methods. He no longer lived in barracks and ate at the cadet mess. He shared a room in bachelor officers' quarters and provided his own meals at officers' club, or, if he wanted to pay for it, in cadet mess. But he had two more schools to go to before he would be a bomber pilot. He had to go to twin-motor school and to four-motor school. In bigger and more complicated ships he had to fly formations and practice missions in the big ships. He had to learn to use four throttles instead of one, and now that he was getting to be a real pilot he didn't think very much about it. He was still a student and the work was constant. He was doing much more than learning a craft and a profession. He was growing into a way of life.

His father wrote to him about the crops and about the Holstein twin calves that had been born. His brother wrote about his marriage and it seemed very remote to Joe. It is not very likely that when the war is over the four-motor pilots will go back to farms and businesses. They will be flying men permanently. The new dimension will be open to them. They will move the produce of the world. Flying will be so deep in them that they will not leave it. In a world which has left wheels for wings they will be the hearts and brains behind the wings. As no other group they will be needed when the war is over.

In the squadron rooms now, they talk of flying and of flying problems. They talk with their hands, thumb against thumb and the fingers spread like wings. The hands are the ship and the little fingers are the ailerons. It is a characteristic gesture. They fly their hands while they talk. Joined hands make dives and climbing turns. There is a close fraternity among pilots and they have their own language and their own set of symbols. To have gone through the schools they must be very good, very intelligent and alert. They carry themselves with poise and confidence. When the four-motor school is finished, when they are at last four-motor bomber men, they fly the great ships—ships that cost a quarter of a million dollars to build and that have all the world knows about flying in their construction and their instrument boards. These men should be confident and proud, for their hands on controls and throttles hold also attack on the enemy and direct defense of the nation.

Other branches of Army and Navy may have complicated actions and tactics designed to win a war, but for all the complication of his training the bomber man's mission is very simple. He must find the enemy and destroy him, whether it be his factories, his troops, his supply lines, or his invasion ships. The history of the Army Air Force is very short. Ships were lost on the ground in the surprise at Pearl Harbor, it is true, but we have never lost an air battle; and on two occasions, in a war that is not yet a year old, the enemy has been met at sea with his strength of escorts and anti-aircraft and fighter planes. The big bombers have come in like avenging birds and they have left a broken, scattered, and distracted enemy. All over the country, in hundreds of schools, the young men are becoming pilots. Every day hundreds of new, raw young men, are shivering with excitement when they climb into the little primary ships, and every day the finished pilots bring down the great bombers and are graduated to their final bomber stations. It is an endless business.

Joe finished his four-motor school and he had a week of furlough. He thought he was very tired, that he would go back to the farm and eat and sleep for a week. He saw sacks of fertilizer in the barn and he saw the twin Holstein calves and the third day he was restless. Every flight of ships that went over the house made him step out to look at and to identify the ships. By ear he tried to call the type and number of ships by the sound of the motors. Before the week was done he was anxious to get back. If he had tried to explain it to himself, there was no one to talk flying to. Later perhaps he would take it easier, would find interests besides flying, but now he was a pilot first and everything else was secondary. He had a sense of elation when his week was up. He wasn't leaving home—he was going home.

THE AERIAL ENGINEER—Crew Chief

PILOT, copilot, navigator, bombardier, gunner. There are two more vital members of a bomber crew, both specialists and experts. These are the aerial engineer and the radio operator. These two are technical sergeants, not commissioned officers, but in the bomber crew they have a standing out of all proportion to their stripes.

The radio man is boss of communications and the engineer is the boss of the engines. As with other members of the crew the nation is fortunate in having a reservoir of men, mechanically-minded and with engine experience. It is not nearly so great a jump from Ford engines to the great power plants of the B-24 as it is from no engine to Ford engine. Training a man who has no experience at all with gasoline engines would be a long job and one which could not turn out experts quickly. But we have a wealth of partly trained men, garage mechanics who know gas engines inside out, high school graduates who have kept the motor running when it should have been dead.

Engines are in the souls of our people. The crew chief will go to school in the Army, it is true, but he is better off if he has some experience with machines before he makes his application for school. Aerial engineers are drawn from the ranks of the Army, both enlisted and drafted men. Their questionnaires will have established whether they have some mechanical experience and their intelligence tests will indicate whether they are of the quality the Air Force insists upon.

Air Force specifications for a crew chief are as follows: The nature of his duties—He flies with multi-engine bombers and transport planes and makes repairs and adjustments during

Washing down a Flying Fortress after a mission

flight; he substitutes for or helps the copilot in operation of
flaps, raising and lowering landing gear, and other mechanical
operations; he serves as aerial gunner during attack, supervises
the ground maintenance of the ship to which he is assigned. He
has gone to Army Air Force school for eighteen weeks and his
training has included basic instructions in materials, care of
equipment, electrical and shock, fundamental airplane structure, hydraulic systems and miscellaneous equipment, propellers, instruments, electrical systems, engines, fuel and oil
systems, engine operation and tests, airplane inspection and
maintenance with both single- and multi-engine planes. He may
be eighteen to forty-four years old. If he is married, he must

The crew chief directs the engine changes of a B-24

sign a statement that his dependents have sufficient means of support. He must have successfully completed the aircraft mechanics courses and have had experience in the mechanics on a bomber. He must have 20, 20 vision without glasses and no color blindness. His hearing must also be 20, 20. His height should be from 60 inches to 76 inches and his weight from 105 lbs. to 200 lbs., depending on how he is built. Although it is not necessary it would be valuable if the applicant for an aerial engineer has studied airplane mechanics, sheet metal, bench metal work, welding, woodworking, mechanical drawing, blueprint reading, pattern making, mathematics including the fundamental processes, equations and formulae, circular and angular measurements, scales, laying out geometrical figures and development, science, including the physical characteristics of materials used in aircraft construction and maintenance, and physical training.

These things are not required, but if the applicant has had some of them it will be much easier for him to go through the Air Force schools. In one sense the aerial engineer is the boss and the nursemaid of the bomber. His okay is necessary before the ship can take off, and the ship's readiness to take off is his responsibility. While the pilot may know a good deal about the engines of the aircraft, the aerial engineer is the true expert and to him all references are submitted. He knows his ship from top to bottom, from propeller to tail. He has his own instrument board for reading the activities of his engines. If an engine should stagger or give trouble in flight he is able to make some repairs before landing.

It is the crew chief, the aerial engineer, who keeps count of the hours on his engines, who directs their removal and replacement when they have fulfilled their time. The crew chief has a unique position in the ship, he is the recognized authority in his field. He has a second duty in action. If the ship is attacking or is attacked, he becomes a gunner. He has been trained to operate the machine gun and he takes his place in the defense of the ship. These are the things a crew chief is supposed to do, but ordinarily he can do much more. It is no unusual thing in our Air Force for a crew chief to be able to fill any position in the ship in an emergency. He has been known to pilot, to navigate, and to bomb. He is that kind of restless intelligent man who learns from anything he touches. The pilot depends upon him greatly, depends upon his judgment and upon his knowledge.

In nearly every small town in America there is a garage run by a natural mechanic. He has usually graduated from high school, and even while he was in school he has repaired auto-

143

A crew chief readies the tail guns of a Flying Fortress for a gunnery mission

mobiles. Such a one was Abner. In his second year in high school he bought two abandoned model T Fords, and using the frame of one, engine block of the other, two wheels from each, he put together a car that would run. But once it was running he was not satisfied, he tinkered with the carburetor until it ran on practically no gasoline. He cut off the fenders and soldered a bullet-shaped body together. For two years he had the car and it was never the same two days in a row. And before he was through he had a fast, smooth-running automobile. Even in high school people sent for him to make little repairs on their cars. He took a correspondence school course in automobile mechanics. When he was out of high school he had already a group of customers and so he opened a little garage in an abandoned blacksmith's shop, dug his own pit and, for that matter, using the repaired blacksmith's forge, made many of his own tools, some of which were more efficient than the ones you buy. Everyone has known a mechanic like Abner, long chin, muscular body, gray eyes, straight blond hair. People trusted Abner to do anything, he was a wizard with an automobile. His bills were reasonable and fair. When he had little work to do he made tools and played with an engine and put it together. He never had time to be married but thought he would someday, if he thought of it at all. His hands, cracked from gasoline and oil, were curiously delicate and his fingers were deft. Boys brought their broken bicycles to Abner to be welded and once he built in a few hours a homemade iron lung for a child suffering from infantile paralysis—and it worked too.

When a customer brought a car to Abner's dark garage he usually stayed around a while to watch the work, for the mechanic personalized his work. He talked to motors, questioned them. He started the motors and listened and he could tell a great deal about a motor by listening to it. It is doubtful whether Abner had much ambition for money or position. He studied constantly, but it wasn't really study. He just wanted to know about mechanical things. When Abner enlisted in the Army, a month after war was declared, his little community in California was upset. Who would repair bicycles? To whom could you take a car and know it would get the best treatment? Who would make a carrying brace so that you could put a canoe on top of a sedan? A customer asked Abner why he had enlisted. Abner wasn't much for such talk. He said helplessly, "Well, we've got a war and—you know they're putting 2,000-horsepower motors in those big bombers? God almighty, I'd like to see those engines."

He enlisted in the Army and questionnaires and tests moved him to the Air Force; and hard as the work was it is doubtful if Abner ever had a better time in his life than at the Army schools. Here for the first time he had the finest engines in the world to play with. He had that certainty in his work which is called authority and he was early slated to be a crew chief. He had confidence in his ability and he gave everyone else confidence in him. On the ground he got his corporal's stripes and then he began to work on the ships and he became a sergeant.

He was bound to be an aerial engineer, a crew chief. He was the proper kind of man for the job. Given work to do in the air it is doubtful whether he would be aware of it being off the ground. His careful hands and good eyes made him an expert gunner. And besides all this he commanded instant respect as a crew chief must. He wanted to know things. He studied navigation in his spare time and he copiloted ships occasionally. Abner is no ideal figure. He is the best possible kind of a crew chief, but he is not an uncommon man. He is, however, primarily and almost uniquely an American kind of a man. Nearly every town has its Abner. The children know him and the boys with their old cars ask his advice. He is a simple man as a good scientist must be. He is a humble man but he will take no nonsense from anyone.

In the Air Force, Abner got his wish to associate with the best engines in the world. They were his babies. He had torn them down and inspected every little part. He had heard them when they were happy and his ears could tell him when they were hurt. The pilot of a bomber could rely on him completely. If Abner said the engines were in good shape, they were all right. He was a quiet man. You had to like him for his silence and everyone did. It is probable that only one thing could outrage him, the mistreatment of a fine piece of machinery. In his little town in California he had been an authority in his field and in the Air Force he was an authority. The men called him "Chief" instinctively. The officers wondered what lucky bomber crew would get him permanently. He had a way of caressing an engine lightly with his fingers. He had a way of cocking his head and rubbing his chin while he listened to an engine. But his interest in engines had greatly enlarged. He knew the whole ship now, the hydraulic lifts on the landing gear, the little cables of the controls, the mechanism of the bomb releases. In an emergency he could do anything in the ship, fly it, bomb from it, lay the machine guns, and even navigate. Many a pilot will tell you that a good crew chief is the greatest man in the air, and from his beginning Abner seemed destined to become one of the greatest of crew chiefs. When his study and his training and his practice were done, Abner was ready for his permanent post in a bomber crew.

THE RADIO ENGINEER

THE long-range bomber crew is almost complete now. It has pilotage, navigation, offensive power, and defensive guns and it has engine maintenance in the air. It lacks only its ears and tongue, its ability to hear and to talk. This has not been left until last because it is unimportant. The bomber's radio and its operator are vastly important. In modern air warfare, either offensive or defensive, it is unusual for a ship to act as a unit. Air tactics call for a number of ships to carry out a given design. The whole plan is the unit, not the ship. The moment a bomber leaves the ground it has only one contact with its ground command and with its flying command and that is through its radio. Into the ears of the radio operators come orders, warnings, changes, and out through his radio go reports of missions, dangers which entangle other ships, reconnaissance observations, and position.

This radio man and his instrument are the contact of the ship with the world outside. And with the complication of tactical and group flying his position has become more and more important. He must maintain communications at all times. He must sometimes even repair his set under fire. Like the engineer the radio man is drawn from the ranks of the Army. The reports on his education and his aptitude indicate whether he is well suited for this complex and responsible position. Let us say that in his high school work he has reported that he studied electrical shop or bench metal work, mechanical drawing, blueprint reading, mathematics, or physics. Such a background suggests that he is eligible for Army Air Force radio school. In this country there are many thousands of men who have made radio

148

"The radio man and his instrument are the contact of the ship with the world
outside . . ."

a hobby. The great Radio Hams organization, which has helped
so often in national emergencies, has as members only a small
proportion of the amateur experts available for the Army
schools.

In addition to these there are many thousands more who have
studied radio by correspondence course or have worked in radio
shops, and all of these have a sturdy background for the Air
Force radio school. A radio man may be anywhere between the
ages of eighteen and forty-four. His hearing must be perfect,
but he may wear glasses if they correct his eyesight to normal
vision. If he is married he must sign a statement that his dependents have sufficient means of support. Once chosen he will go

to radio school, and for a little over eighteen weeks he will study his job, radio operating, Morse code, code typing, radio telephone and telegraph procedures, flight operations, direct and alternating current circuits, transmitters, receivers. He will learn the radio compass and he will learn to service and to maintain the equipment he will be required to use.

In addition he will learn gunnery, for everyone in a bomber crew must in some emergencies be a gunner.

Harris was a proper man for Air Force radio. He was graduated from high school, having had some science and having been most interested in the physics of electricity. While he worked in a large chain grocery, he was not content with that. He had wanted to get into radio since he had first left high school. To that end he had taken a mail-order course and later, by persistent saving, had bought and assembled parts for a little short-wave sending and receiving set. And he was licensed to use it. He carried on lengthy conversations with other hams. They were always groping out to the distances, these hams. They would rather hear a dull man from 5,000 miles than an interesting one from 500. A strange brotherhood they were, almost a lodge. Their dearest acquaintances they never saw. A ham who could make an acquaintance in Timbuctu was just twice as fortunate as one who only had friends in Guam. The war, that is, before we got into it, was a sad thing for Harris. One by one his friends were cut off the air by Germany. Some of them told horrible things before their sets went dead. Harris knew better than most what an Axis victory meant to the defeated. When a man was shot Harris sometimes heard about it from another before he went off the air.

When the war was on, Harris spent every hour trying to hear the illegal sets in Germany and Holland and Norway. These men of radio are internationalists as scientists are. Harris hated the Axis not for killing and silencing strangers, but for

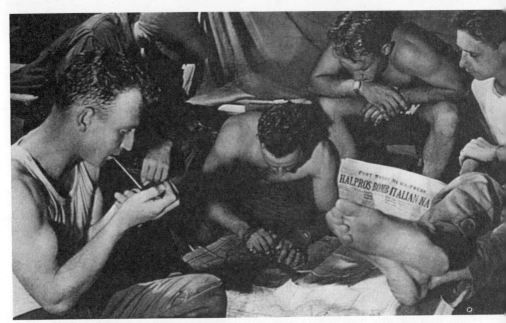
The enlisted men of a bomber crew study navigation in their time off

hurting his friends whose voices he had heard and who had heard his voice. Then we entered the war and Harris surrendered his license. He still listened but he could not send anymore. He had planned to join the Army to get into military radio, but while he was making up his mind his draft board solved the problem for him and he was inducted into the service. His tests and his experience automatically indicated his destiny. He was delighted when he was chosen to go to radio school. With Harris's background it was still hard work, but probably not quite so hard as it was for some of the others. Radio was his first interest in the world and after his eighteen weeks he was graduated and made a technical sergeant.

When the orders came assigning him to a long-range bomber crew he felt savagely good, for he hoped he could help to strike a blow for his friends who had been choked off the air by Germans.

THE BOMBER TEAM

THIS has been an account of the training of the individual members of a bomber crew before they are assembled finally, given their ship, their group training, and their mission. But the air crew is not cut off from the ground crew. Necessity and intelligence have created a relationship between men in the Air Force which is unique in the armed forces. The necessity lies here—an individual in artillery, if he fails in his duty, may be responsible for a shell missing a target. The responsibility of an officer of infantry is much greater than that of a private. But in the Air Force the error or dereliction of a ground crew man, his failure to carry out his job intelligently, can bring a ship crashing down as surely as a bad pilot can, and a crashed ship and a dead crew is a terrible loss.

In this book the point has been made again and again that the Air Force takes only the best men of brain and nerve and judgment and body. It is for the reason that every member of the Air Force must take a great deal of responsibility. A weak link cannot be permitted in the chain for the chain is too interrelated. And with this necessary delegation of responsibility there goes a relationship and a respect which are also unique in the Air Force.

A commissioned flying officer, knowing that his mission and even his life are in the hands of each member of the whole group, is not likely to become the self-sufficient martinet. It wouldn't work. The Air Force is an association of experts and each must place a dependence on the other. In military formation and discipline, men and officers act with precision and snap, but in mission their actions are more likely to be like the work of a fine construction crew. Their discipline is more likely to be the result of the wills of a number of intelligent men all going the same way. It is impossible in the Air Force blindly to carry out an order. If you don't know what you are doing you can't do it. This fact makes for a very different relation between men and officers than has obtained in many military organizations. The old-time soldier would say that discipline would disappear under such a system, but actually the opposite is true. It can be suspected that the old iron discipline helped to conceal from the private soldier the incapacity of the officer, but the Air Force cannot have bad officers or the ships do not fly. The private knows that his officer is an expert in his field and his discipline is that of trust. The officer knows what depends on the private's work and his discipline is one of respect for his men.

The bomber crew is a team in a true sense but it is also true that the whole Air Force is a team. This relationship has not been accidental, it has been carefully planned and carried out by the commanding officers who know how much is at stake. These men being flying officers know what it takes to keep a ship in the air. First and most important of all, it takes the best possible human material, second, complete training of that material, and third, individual and group initiative. It must not be thought that discipline is lax. In effect, it is stricter than in most branches of the Service. But in the Air Forces discipline is defined as that conduct of the individual which in a group best carries out the missions. And blind, unreasoning, unintelligent obedience does not accomplish this definition. A man must be good to get into the Air Force at all, but once in and trained his goodness is recognized and used. That is the strength and certainty of Air Force discipline. Every man is responsible to and for the team, not in fear of punishment nor hope of reward—team play is something far different from that.

A bomber crew approaches its ship for a mission

Every week the Air Force schools all over the country are graduating their specialists. From a four-motor school in Texas a class of pilots comes, from New Mexico bombardiers, from Nevada gunners, navigators from Kelly Field, radio operators from South Dakota, crew chiefs from Illinois or Mississippi. Their individual training period is over and their final training is ready to begin. They will be trained as units in a tight, clannish organization—the bomber crew.

This crew, once established, will remain as a unit. The men will know one another as few men ever get acquainted, for they will be under fire together. They will play together after a victory. They will plan together and eat and sleep together on missions. And finally there is the chance that they may die together. The ties between members of the bomber team are tighter than those of nearly any organization in the world. There must be respect and liking among the men. One ill-fitting man can throw out the smoothness of operation. Dislike may split a crew. This crew must function like a fine watch. One slow or rusty part could make the whole crew bad—such are the complications of human relationships. Relationships are a part of the final training of the group, the getting acquainted, the working together under conditions which are like those they will find on their deadly missions. And when the crew is established and in working shape, the gunners will think their pilot is the best pilot in the Air Force. The pilot will tell anyone that there is no crew chief like his and he will give examples and prove it. The crew will be a tight unit, a jealous unit. Their feeling will not be loud nor boastful, nor even stated unless one member is criticized, but the feeling will be there. And this fierce, inner loyalty extends to the ships. A bomber crew which uses the Flying Fortress, the B-17E, will feel that there is no ship like it. The crew of the Consolidated B-24 will be just as partial to its ship. This is a curious thing. The ships are about equal in performance and yet each one has its passionate adherents. And individual ships are personalized too, are given names and even unconsciously thought of as persons. No amount of precision, mass production manufacture, can remove the personalities from the ships. No two ships fly quite alike, each one has its personality to be learned in the controls by pilot and copilot and in feel by the rest of the crew. The ship is the center of the bomber crew. They will spend many hours in her. She is a part of the crew too.

So, to the assembly field come the men and they are fitted together. The commissioned officers live together and the non-commissioned officers live together. At present there are no privates in a bomber crew. When they have learned enough to be there, rank and pay have been increased. Gunners, radio men, crew chiefs are sergeants drawing specialist's pay and flying pay. Pilot and copilot, bombardier, and navigator are commissioned officers. The men live together, go out together, eat together. They fly individual missions, flight missions, squadron missions. If an animosity should arise, here in final training is the place to root it out. Here develop close associations, friendships that are permanent; and it must be that way, for rigid discipline can never take the place of mutual liking and respect. There are more musketeers here than the original three, but the motto of a bomber crew might well be the familiar "All for one and one for all." Men who know what they are doing are the best fighting instruments in the world. Nothing manufactured can take their place. Men are the true weapons of the Air Force and it is an understanding of this that makes our bomber crews what they are. It is an understanding of this which goes into the careful choice of candidates, the careful training of individuals, and finally, the careful grouping of the men in the crew.

The men graduate from the schools and they get their orders and usually a little furlough, for they have worked long and hard. Before the furlough is up they are restless. A place without airplanes is no longer a good place to them. They do not rest well if the sound of ships on the runway is not in their ears. They are trained for a job and with very few exceptions they want to get to their job.

This final phase of training will simulate battle conditions in every possible way. The crews will bomb targets in the water, they will be given patrol missions, and if they are lucky they may get a submarine. Each man has been thinking in terms of his specialty, but now each will begin to think in terms of the mission. The word mission will change its meaning. Mission is the end toward which they have been working. A mission will be the most important thing in the world to them. On the field they will get to know men of more advanced squadrons and then one day these squadrons will be gone giving no destination; but the crews that are left will read newspapers and sometimes an oblique piece of information will tell them where their friends are.

Training, bombing, getting used to the ship and to their duties in the ship go on and on. The group will be a unit. And then one day a stir of excitement will run through the squadron —the orders are in. It is time to pack up. It is time to go. They do not yet know where. They may go any place toward which the compass can point. The men move about quickly. The ships are packed. Squadron records are boxed. Then final orders come and quietly the men take their places, the engines turn over. The ships rumble out to the runway. Then the ground shakes under the spinning wheels and the air roars with the motors. The mission has begun.

It happened that Bill the bombardier, Joe the pilot, Al the gunner, Harris the radio man, Abner the engineer, and Allan the navigator all finished their training at the same time. Hundreds finished at that time and received their orders to proceed to their final training, but these were ordered to a field in Florida. They came in on the train and shortly were assigned to their squadrons and flights. The commanding officer had observed the men carefully. In case he made a mistake in building the crews it could be changed but it is better not to make a mistake. He assigned the men to a crew together with a copilot and two other gunners. This was the crew and it was to be permanent.

It was hot at the field and damp, and millions of mosquitoes hummed about day and night. The men slept in shelters open all the way around but tightly screened. But even then some mosquitoes got in and many little black bugs walked through the meshes of the screen at will. Fanciers of bugs that bite favor the black bugs over the mosquitoes as unpleasant visitors. For a mosquito must find an exposed place to bite, but the black bugs go right under the covers with you. For a few days the new men fought and slapped the bugs and finally they gave up and relaxed and the bugs bit them and they didn't suffer so much.

The field had been built quickly, leveled quickly. Shelters were still going up. The air was thick and humid and pools of water were everywhere. If it was a toughening process in discomfort it was successful. The nearest town was five miles away. It was not the Florida that the Chambers of Commerce talk about. The field itself had been torn and chewed by the bulldozers out of a palmetto swamp, leveled, and the asphalt runways laid down, and around the field, well spaced, stood the brown B-24's like giant mosquitoes.

In the operations room the new crew stood about a little diffidently. Their shirts were sweated through, their faces ran with perspiration. They had been told to get acquainted. They examined one another secretly. They were a little embarrassed and then outside and on the other side of the field a motor turned over and caught and another and two more. The new crew moved as one man to the open door and looked across the field to where a bomber was warming up. They could see the crew of that ship climbing in, taking their sheepskin clothes, their masks, and their parachutes with them. And Bill said "They're going high."

"It will be cool up there, anyway," said Allan.

The strangeness wore off in a very few days and when the nine of them got into a ship together for the first time, it disappeared. On their first flight they tried to do their best. Abner went over his motors on the ground and hovered about like a worried hen. He hesitated to report the engines ready for fear

158

Flying Fortress takes off on a practice mission

he might have missed something. Joe took his place. Harris was working at his radio set, sitting in his swinging chair behind the copilot. The gunners were in the section behind the bomb bays for the take-off and Allan and Bill had their seats on the left side. They would both go into the nose of the ship as soon as she was in the air. Abner came aboard through the open bomb bay and as soon as he was on, the doors rolled shut. Joe leaned out of his window, "Clear number one."

"Clear," the ground sergeant said. The three-bladed propeller turned jerkily, once, twice, fired and caught and Joe idled it back. "Clear number two," and number two caught. Three and four started. Abner sighed with nervous relief. Bill put on his

159

earphones and lifted his microphone. He got his clearance from operations. He taxied the ship to the runway, set the brakes, and reversed each engine while the ship strained at the brakes. Then Joe called the tower and reported himself ready and was cleared. His hands pushed the four red-headed throttle handles forward, the engines strained to get away and could not, so they took the ship with them. The great ship thundered down the runway, 60, 70, 80 and at 90 Joe pulled back gently and the great brown bomber lifted into the air. Abner came forward and pulled the levers which lifted the wheels into the slots in the wings.

Now Allan and Bill climbed through the narrow passage from the bomb bay to the nose. The navigator's table was there and a swinging chair for the bombardier. Bill leaned over his bombsight and glanced up at his instrument panel. Allan laid out his maps on the table and took the cover off his compass. Now the gunners took their places. Al crawled into the tail gun turret and the second gunner stepped across the catwalk and took his place in the glistening, transparent top turret. The third gunner stayed close to the belly turret. If he could put the cross hairs of his sights on an enemy and pull his trigger, two streams of steel would pour from his guns into the enemy ship. This was their first flight together. They made a short navigational flight out over the Gulf of Mexico.

They were to get used to their ship and to each other. Below them on the smooth sea they could watch the cargo ships moving and they knew that submarines were waiting somewhere. Their orders were to fly a hundred miles out to sea and then to turn and make twelve bombing runs over a floating target. The position of the target was given, but Allan had to find it with his instruments. He sat at his table looking worried and now and then calling a direction into his microphone to Joe.

The ship flew easily without much noise. The copilot was leaning forward watching the gauges. The altimeter showed

160

Sitting in the glass nose of a bomber, the navigator guides the ship in its over-water patrol

10,000 feet and that was on their orders. Suddenly in the earphones came Bill's excited voice.

"Joe, look down about 127 degrees and see what you think that is."

Joe put the ship into a turn so he could look down from his window. Far below he could see a little trail of white water and under it a long, thin shadow. Joe lifted his microphone. "Harris," he said, "get the tower, report a submarine." The little wake was far behind now. Joe cut his motor and he began to lose altitude. He heard the voice of the squadron radio operator saying, "Hold it, one moment," and then his squadron leader.

"We have no submarines in the area. If you've got live bombs go after it. What's the position?" Joe gave him the position. "Okay, we'll send the depth charges, you try them with bombs."

Joe said, "Wilco," but his voice was tight. "Did you hear that, Bill?"

"I heard it."

"You better come in as low as you can, I'll drop a salvo."

Joe said, "You better hit him, we've only got one chance. He can get down like a flash." He called the tail gunner, "We're going after a submarine, watch as we go over. You might give him something if we miss."

"Okay," said Al.

The ship made a turn, and with motors idling dropped quietly towards the little splash of wake in the distance. From the nose Bill directed the flight.

"A little left now, hold it, hold it." Then he cried, "I think they're coming up." The copilot leaned forward tensely. Abner stood holding on to the structure of the top turret.

"Get down," Bill called. "Get down another thousand feet."

The ship settled fast. They could hear the bomb bay doors slide up like the top of a roll-top desk. Bill's voice was cracked with excitement.

162

"Two points left, hold it steady right there now."

Then they heard the metallic spit as the salvo went out and Bill shouted, "Bombs away." And it was hardly shouted before the explosion came and the ship lurched under the air pressure. The tail gun was banging away behind. Joe whirled the ship up on its side to see. There were pieces of superstructure still in the air when he looked and Bill was shouting:

"He was coming up! We got him!"

Joe speeded his engines, gained altitude, and continued the circle. The spot on the sea was still torn with white water and a spread of shimmering oil was edging out from the disturbance.

Joe lifted his microphone. "Bill," he said, "if you'd missed, we'd have killed you. Harris, call the squadron and report a direct hit and the submarine sunk and repeat the position."

A moment later he heard the squadron leader, "Good work. Continue on your mission. Any bombs left?"

"No, sir, we dropped both racks."

"Well, make four dry runs over the target then."

"Roger," said Joe, and he hung his microphone on its clamp. His hands were steady but he seemed to be jumping and pulsing inside. In the nose Bill turned and smiled happily at the navigator and then he leaned over and kissed the bombsight.

When they came in—when Joe let the ship down on the squalling wheels and dropped in the protesting nose wheel— they had gotten themselves in hand enough so that they could be nonchalant. It had been pure luck, they knew, but they liked pure luck. So many people speak of luck disparagingly, as though it weren't a good thing to have. This crew was quiet about the submarine. Each one of course under pressure would tell about it, would tell his version of it, but the most important thing of all was that this crew was now a crew. In one action it had welded together. Very strange ties had been established. These men would not be apart again. On the surface the pilot

163

knew he had a good bombardier; the bombardier knew that he had the best of pilots. But beyond this there were bonds of relationship extending through the whole ship. The submarine belonged to the crew. The team was a unit.

On the ground Bill packed up his bombsight and marched it away under guard. The crew, all except Abner, walked in with the parachutes. There was something they wanted to do now, something bomber crews usually do when they come back from a successful action. They would go into town and have dinner together, all of them, but with no one else. They would drink a few glasses of beer and then they would sit back and discuss the action, but no stranger would be there, just the crew.

They had to wait a while for Abner. He was all over the engines with a ground crew. He thought the landing gear had been slow coming down. He was sure he had heard a complaint in number three engine. While they waited for Abner, Joe made his report and turned it in. Finally, there were clean, fresh uniforms and they rode a bus into town. They went to a restaurant and got a private room and when they were seated, Bill raised his beer glass. "Well," he said, "well, here's luck."

The crew soon found that the lucky finding and sinking of a submarine is not air warfare. They went up in group flights. They flew in echelons of units. The missions were long and constant. They went out on patrol, flew over Cuba and Haiti and back by way of the bulge of Yucatan. The trips were very long. The gunners soon learned to sleep until they were called. Flying low in the hot Gulf air, they took off most of their clothes, and flying and bombing, from 25,000, they wore sheepskins and masks, for the temperature was 40 degrees below zero, and the air was thin.

The missions were exact representations of active warfare. The flights were planned and carried out with every attention to detail.

164

A bomber crew returns from a mission

Living and working together, they played together too. On the beach in their free time they played football and swam in the warm water of the Gulf. Pilot and copilot, bombardier and navigator rented a house near the field and cooked their dinners there sometimes. In the quarters Harris and Abner were studying aerial navigation at night. Daily the missions grew more complex. Exact attack conditions were given and there really

165

"On the beach in their free time they play football . . ."

were submarines in the Gulf. Night missions and day missions, practice at finding and bombing an enemy fleet. The orders would be something like this:

"Intelligence Estimate of the Situation. Mission No. 4, the date. 1. Enemy situation—Enemy submarines were sighted off the coast of Cayo Romano at an approximate position of North 22 degrees latitude in the old Bahama channel. A fleet of enemy surface craft were reported to be further to the Southeast in battle formation. 2. Mission—to track down any enemy craft, surface or submerged, and destroy upon sight. 3. Formation and route—the——group will proceed in vee formation of two ships per element from——Field with the——bomb squadron

166

leading. At 25 degrees North latitude and 80 degrees East latitude, the vee formation will give way to an extended search formation and fly down the San Paren channel. Where the San Paren meets the Nicholas channel, the formation will make a 135 degree turn to the East and proceed down the old Bahama channel to the general vicinity of Cayo Romano. At this point the formation will execute a turn of 180 degrees and proceed up the old Bahama channel into Nicholas channel. Before crossing the 81st meridian of latitude, the formation will make a 115 degree turn and head straight North to Florida. Upon sighting land the search formation will go back to the original vee and proceed to the home base, where they will stand by for further mission."

These would be the orders for a mission and on the return of the formation, a report would be made that went something like this:

"At approximately 0915, the ships took off from——for the scheduled mission. After circling the field, the ships fell into vee formation and proceeded upon a Southeasterly course (135 degrees true course). This was followed for approximately 150 miles until the base point (25 degrees 00 minutes North and 80 degrees 00 minutes West) was reached. Just before reaching the base point, a coastal air patrol plane was spotted some 15 miles from shore and headed landward. The ship was a yellow, single-engine monoplane flying at 2500 feet engaged in observation. It was sighted at approximately 1045.

"The base point was reached at 1054 and the formation broke from the conventional vee to extended search formation. The flight continued in this fomation until mainland was again reached on the return trip.

"At 1015, a B-17E was sighted flying over the formation at an altitude of 2500 feet. Its marking was reported to be No. 1002 and the ship flew at an approximate course of 300 degrees.

167

"A single-stack steamer was sighted at 1059 to the East of the formation. The ship sailed on a course of 340 degrees at an approximate speed of 20 knots. All the coral reefs (Dog Rocks, Damas Cays, and the Auguile Isles) sighted along the San Paren channel were reported by the formation.

"The flight continued on the scheduled route, but no enemy submarines nor surface craft were sighted anywhere in the vicinity of the designated area.

"At 1220 the formation made a 180-degree turn at Cayo Paredon and proceeded back by way of the old Bahama channel and Nicholas channel. Sailboats were reported to be in the area of Cayo Coco, Cayo Caiman, and Cayo Fragoso. From 1315 to 1330, three Navy ships were sighted off the coast of Cayo Hical and Crisco. Reports conflict as to their type. The majority of the reports seem to indicate the ships to be Navy tankers.

"At 1400 a rendezvous was held 8 miles Northeast of Oyster Key to enable all the ships from the search formation to fall into the conventional vee formation. Home base was sighted at 1458 and the ships of the——bombardment squadron left the remainder of the ships of the group to proceed to their home base for further operations. Approved by the squadron commander."

Such was the report of a mission and it contained all the information necessary, but it did not tell how they flew over the sighted ships while the Naval gunners watched them and the crews waved at them; and the report did not tell how, when they flew over the little green islands, they could see children rush out of the houses to look up at the bombers, not in fear but in pride. The crews of the bombers peered down, trying to see the shape of a submarine in the water. They knew that they had to look for little more than shadows, for submarines in these waters are painted white so that they may lie on the sand bottom unobserved in the daytime.

It was a working crew now and it was rapidly learning its

A bomber crew learns how to identify all types of airplanes

business. One day an alert was ordered and gas masks issued. It was very hot. Even the gas masks were hot against a man's side. Al the gunner left his mask in the squadron room and walked out on the field when the gas raid came. A flight of ships went over and thoroughly drenched the field with tear gas. Al ran for his mask trying to hold his breath, but he could not make it and he was choking and weeping when he got to his gas mask and weakly put it on. The raid was necessary. No one would ever forget his mask again.

The crew had learned the ship now and they had named her *Baby,* had painted the name on her nose. Bill designed a picture for the nose, a plummeting figure, half bomb and half bathing girl, speeding downward. *Baby* was their ship and they felt that in some ways she was superior to other ships, just as they felt that their crew was a little bit better than other crews. They were real bombardment men now. They scanned the newspapers. Reports were beginning to be published about the work of American ships already overseas in action.

Midway was their battle now and the Coral Seas and Tobruk. They knew that ships like *Baby* were flying out of England already to bomb the production of Germany. Often they discussed the question of where they would be sent—to Australia to carry the war to the Japanese, to Africa to break up Rommel's supplies, to England to strike out at Germany. If they had had free choice they would have chosen two targets, Berlin and Tokyo. But these were token places and *Baby's* men knew now what air war is. A munitions plant destroyed is more important than a capitol bombed. They knew the mathematics of destruction. Guns and ammunition and food that does not arrive is more important than a bomb dropped in the Wilhelmstrasse. Perhaps the Germans could stand the bombing of Berlin and perhaps they could not, no one knows. But Germans nor anyone else can fight without food and ammunition. That we do know.

Joe wondered how he would feel when anti-aircraft was firing at *Baby* and when the fighters jabbed at her. He didn't know. He knew that other pilots were doing very well and he thought he might not fall too far short when the time came.

The time was coming soon, they knew that. The tempo of training was stepping up. The squadron leader grew more and more critical of everything but perfect bombing. Since *Baby's* crew had come they had seen two squadrons leave, at least they had heard them leave, for they disappeared at night and left no word of their destination, and new squadrons had come to take their places in the training.

All of the training was pyramiding toward this point of departure on real mission. Mission became almost a mystic word. Mission was the reason for all the complex and complicated training they had been through. They were a unit now, tighter knit than any group they had ever known.

A B-24 is gassed up for a mission

MISSIONS

BEFORE describing various missions assigned to the bomber team whose training we have followed in these pages, it might be well to look into the organization of the Air Force units and so understand how missions are planned and from where orders for them are issued.

To most people the units of the Army are well known, the corps, the brigade, the regiment, the battalion, the company, and the squad are very familiar. Perhaps the units of the Air Force are not quite so well known. It might be well here briefly to describe those units. The largest unit in the Air Force is the Wing and it would correspond roughly to a brigade in the land Army. It is the largest air fighting unit which one commander can efficiently control and directly supervise. In *Winged Warfare* by General Arnold and General Eaker, the following explanation is given of the organization of the Air Force. Of the Wing, they say: "It is a tactical command as differentiated from an administrative command. The Wing Commander supervises the training and tactical operations of his groups and is not concerned primarily with administration and supply. These latter functions are performed by air base groups which are housed in peacetime on air bases with the tactical groups and which perform their administrative, supply and housekeeping functions for them."

The next unit under the Wing is the Air Force Group which is usually composed of three squadrons. Again quoting *Winged Warfare:* "It was conceived as the largest air unit which one leader can efficiently control in the air. Tactical Groups are for the most part heterogeneous in that their three component

172

The Commanding Officer of a Bombardment Group

squadrons will be of the same tactical type, that is fighter or bombardment. The Group corresponds to the regiment. It is both a tactical and an administrative unit. Its commander is generally of the rank of Colonel or Lieutenant Colonel and is always an experienced flying officer who is capable of leading his unit in air combat as compared to one who directs his command from the ground. The bombardment group, for example, is composed of 60 officers and 800 men. It has attached small units of ordnance, signal, and medical troops for service in the field. In addition, forward echelons of the air base units perform its housekeeping and airdrome functions when it is in the theater of operations. While stationed at a permanent air base, the air base group for that station performs these service functions for the combat group.

"The squadron is the air unit corresponding to the battalion in ground arms. It is commanded by a major and is the basic flying combat unit. Squadrons of various types have different composition. For instance, a fighter squadron is composed of twenty-eight officers and 150 men and has for equipment 28 planes, while a bomber squadron has 21 officers, 180 men, and 13 planes. The squadron is deemed essential as is the battalion in the infantry, in order to have a unit sufficiently small in size to receive personal supervision, direction and control of one experienced officer and in order to provide for detailed training and first-hand direction of supply, discipline and combat methods. Squadron commanders are always flying officers of long experience and are selected for executive ability in the supervision of training and combat leadership. There are six types of combat squadrons with slightly different organization and personnel strength, dependent upon the type of aircraft they fly. These are transports; fighter; light; medium and heavy bombardment and reconnaissance."

To the member of the bomber crew, the squadron is the personal and familiar unit. He knows his squadron leader and his squadron leader knows him. It is in the squadron room where flight plans are made and where experiences are retailed after the mission. Group and wing are as remote as regiment and brigade are to the common soldier. The squadron leader has a very close and personal contact with his men, and being a flying officer he has their respect, for it is obvious that he knows a little more about operations than they do. In most cases the squadron leader is more than a military leader to his squadron. He is the source of advice and in many cases the custodian of the secrets of many of his men. The squadron leader is the pivot of liaison between the higher command and the units of the Air Force. He must have genuine administrative ability, but in addition to this he must have the common touch and the genuine force of leadership to weld the complex personalities of all of his unit men into a unit squadron. The squadron is movable. It keeps the records of individuals, it issues the orders, it recommends promotion, and prescribes punishment. From the standpoint of the men, the squadron is the most important unit in the Air Force.

Baby's pilot and copilot, bombardier and navigator went to the squadron room under orders and they found the crews of five other ships there. The squadron leader, a major of forty-two, sat behind his desk. "You're going on a night mission," he said, "a bomber flight of six planes. The target is a barge anchored in the Gulf. Now, here are the maps." The pilots leaned close over the operations table and studied the position of the target. They worked out their flight plans as they had been taught.

"The only thing there won't be is anti-aircraft and enemy fighters, but make sure your gunners are alert and that they keep their sights warm. Better get some sleep now. The start is eleven exact."

It was not a nice night. Loose, low clouds hung at 1,200 feet

175

and sent down a warm drizzle. The airfield was dark. One had to go close to see the sentries about the ships. The men drew their sheepskin clothes, loose pants, and jackets of lambskin with the fleece inside and they drew oxygen masks and parachutes and fleece-lined boots. Containers of hot coffee went aboard the ships and boxes of sandwiches. At 1055 Bill went to the ship with his guarded bombsight. The ground crews were working on the motors, filling the gas tanks, and the bomb crews were loading 100 lb. bombs into the open bellies of the ships and locking them in the bomb racks. Allan looked nervously at his map. The gunners were in the ship checking their ammunition. At 1058 Joe and Allan and Harris went out to *Baby*. Abner was hovering about with the ground crew. Bill checked the bombs and inspected the bomb latches in the racks. Then the engines started and idled in the darkness. At 11 sharp the flight leader moved out to the runway. His ship roared down the asphalt, shooting sparks from its exhaust, and it took the air. *Baby* was right behind. Joe looked at the second hand of his stop watch. When it crossed the one minute mark he pushed his throttles ahead, roared down the dark runway and lifted into the air. The other ships came behind, each one a minute behind the other. *Baby* bounced up into the clouds and lost sight of everything till at 10,000 feet she burst out into a clear dark night littered with stars. Allan called the course. They were to rendezvous at 1145 at a spot over the ocean to be found in the dark, by instruments. Time, speed, altitude, all were calculated. *Baby* had to be there within a very few seconds. Bill lifted the ship to 15,000 feet. The radio was dead on this mission. Harris had his set open but he was not talking. Abner moved sleekly about testing the de-icers, turning the valves of the oxygen tubes. They were to rendezvous at 18,000 feet.

At 15,000, Joe spoke into his microphone to the crew. They slipped into sheepskins and boots and adjusted the oxygen masks, fitted the rubber tubes to the copper supply tubes. It was cold in the ship, a little frost began to form on the edges of the wings. Abner started the de-icing pumps. The rubberwing edges pulsed, shook off the first ice. Allan at his little table worked on the course. A small shaded globe threw a round spot of light on his table. He called into his microphone and the co-pilot raised the ship's nose for more altitude. Joe was out of his seat slipping on his sheepskins. When he was back and strapped in, Abner brought him a paper cup of hot coffee. It was very cold in the ship. The only light on Baby was a dim running light arear and on top of the fuselage. Joe could not see any of the other ships. At 1143 Allan began to lean forward and peer out of the nose of the ship. Joe checked his watch.

At 1145 exactly he saw a flash of wing lights ahead, a quick flash, and he said quietly into his microphone, "Good work, Allan." Allan heaved a great sigh of relief. It is something to find a spot that doesn't exist except on your instruments.

The other ships were there at the same moment. The last ship had come in at an advanced speed. He had come just six minutes quicker than the flight commander. *Baby* took her place to the right and above and behind the leader. There was another ship to the right above and behind *Baby*. On the other, the left leg of the vee, were two more ships, while the sixth ship flew behind and between the spread legs of the vee. Each ship watchd the dim light of the ship ahead. The pilots carefully maintained the intervals. The flight went up to 25,000 feet now and the men needed the oxygen. The ships flew on and on into the dark night. Below, the clouds thinned and they could see patches of dark ocean. The men sat quietly in the darkened ships.

Only a little glow came from the instrument panels where the dials were lighted. At one o'clock the flight leader's wing lights flashed. Joe leaned forward. The signal came then to attack. Joe pulled back his throttles and the roaring motors

The bombardier at his post for a night flight

quieted. The ships dropped back in a line about a mile apart and began to lose altitude. In the nose, Bill took the cover from his bombsight, cleaned his eyepiece with a handkerchief. The bomb bay doors rolled up and the ship dropped slowly. They could not see the leader's lights now. Allan, with the target spotted on his map, called the course. The oxygen masks came off now. The gunners sat up straight in their stations. Bill strained his eyes forward into the darkness.

Allan said into his microphone, "Nearly there," and then below them and far ahead there was a flash of light and another and another. Three flares dropped by the leader floated down on parachutes and ahead and below on the surface of the water, Bill could see the target barge with a white cross painted on it. He leaned low over his bombsight and his fingers worked busily at the knobs. The barge was on the cross hairs. He pressed the release and sat back. Five seconds, ten, fifteen, and the whisking sound as the bomb train went out, not in salvo all at once but each one a fraction of a second behind the other. Bill looked down and back now. He could not see his bombs falling but he saw the line of flashes as the train marched over the target, and the flashes had hardly stopped before a second line of bursts from the ship behind trooped over. Four trains were released and the last ship took the photographs of a wrecked and sinking target.

And now the signal came from the leader to go home. Joe looked at his watch. The return was just as carefully plotted but it was a scattered return and the ships must land at one-minute intervals at the field from which they had taken off.

Allan still worked at his table. It was just as hard getting back as going out. The runway of an airfield is a very small place to find on the surface of the earth. They landed at last and saw that the propellers of the leader's ship were still turning on the flight line. Joe brought his ship in and taxied off the runway just as the third ship came in. The crew climbed out. They were tired from the strain of trying to do the job perfectly, and although they did not know how they knew it, each man knew that the last practice flight was over. The apprenticeship was done. Their next flight would be to a battle station somewhere in the world.

Bill and Joe and Allan talked it over the next morning. They were frying eggs and ham for their breakfast. The night flight meant they did not have to report until 3 o'clock in the afternoon. They knew their training was over. They were a bombardment unit now. This crew gathered from so many places, from so many different backgrounds, was a crew now, molded and trained to do a job. They had no patriotic sentiments. Those were for politicians. They were workmen, specialists. If the safety and future of the country depended on them, you could not learn that from them. They thought in terms of distance and of course and of demolition. They thought in terms of calibers and horsepower, of lift and range, and right now they thought in terms of ham and eggs and coffee. But the great mission was in their heads.

Bill said, "Hey, Joe, you got any idea where we'll go?"

And Joe said, "Sure, England or India or Africa or maybe China or Alaska."

"No, seriously Joe, don't you know?"

"No," said Joe, "but I'll be awful glad to get going. I used to run in school. You get down on your mark and you wait for the gun. That's a funny time while you're waiting for the gun."

"Well, I hope they shoot her pretty soon."

Bill said, "Suppose we will get any leave before we take off?"

"How do I know?" Joe went on mumbling into a mouthful of ham.

The crew knew they were going and the whole field knew it although there were no orders yet. *Baby's* crew belonged to the

180

Navigator, bombardier, and pilot of a bomber crew

senior squadron on the field. New squadrons were behind them now and they had seen other squadrons go ahead of them.

In the newspapers there were constant reports. A flight of B-24's had bombed Tobruk. Another flight had reduced German shipping to wreckage in a port of Greece. They wondered if these could be men they knew. They might be the men they had eaten with in town and had played pool with in the B O Q. Abner went out that morning with a can of white paint and he freshened the name *Baby* on the ship and he went over the outlines of the insignia, a bathing girl built like a bomb plummeting downwards.

The time was coming. The squadron knew it. Daily, nightly, the missions went out over the Gulf, but the big mission was coming. The mission toward which all the training had aimed—contact with the enemy, a well-armed, well-trained desperate enemy. That was why the men looked so carefully at the newspapers and what they found in the newspapers reassured them. Our ships are as good or better than anything in the world. Our crews are better. They found in the papers that when forces were equal, our force won.

The major called the pilots in and fifteen minutes later they came out of the squadron room.

Bill said "We going?"

"Yes," said Joe.

"When?"

"Tonight."

"You know where?"

"No. You want to get your things together," Joe said.

"That won't take half an hour." And then Joe said, "You can write some letters. They'll be posted after we go."

And each man wrote his letters home. They were not the kind of letters they could have written six months before.

In the late evening the bomber sits quietly waiting for its crew

Bill wrote, "I'm sorry I won't be able to go quail hunting this season, but I guess we'll be going hunting all right."

And Joe wrote, "And now might be a good time to buy a few sows. Pork will probably bring a good price this year. I'll write when I know where we are." They wrote quiet, matter-of-fact letters and they put them in the box to be mailed after they had gone. The men felt matter-of-fact. It is always like that just before action. All the churning and expectations and the tremors go away and, well, there is a job to do, a ship to fly, bombs to drop. *Baby's* crew got ready quietly. They packed their bags, shirts, socks, and underwear, toothbrushes. There wasn't much besides these things. They had not had time to accumulate things. Accumulation takes leisure.

On the field they met men from other squadrons. "I hope we'll join you before long," they said. It was a very quiet time that afternoon. This cross section, these men from all over the country, from all the background of the country, had become one thing—a bomber crew. They were changed but they had not lost what they were, they were still individuals. Perhaps that is what makes our crews superior. The split seconds where a man's judgment is the most important thing in the world. They did not think how important they were to the nation. It is doubtful that they even knew it.

In the afternoon they shaved and cleaned up and went to dinner all together and when they sat down Joe lifted his beer glass, but all he could think to say was "Well, here's luck!"

In the dark they went out to *Baby* where she stood in the line. There were no lights. The crew clambered in through the open bomb bay. Joe, the pilot from South Carolina, and Bill from Idaho and Allan from Indiana and Abner from California. Their luggage was stowed in the big compartment back of the bomb bays. They buckled on their parachutes, snapped their safety belts. Allan waited in his take-off seat with his map case

184

in his hand. The squadron leader's motors started. Joe leaned out of his window. "Clear number one," he called and from the darkness "number one clear" came back. The engines started. Abner cocked his head, the better to hear them. Bill sat in his take-off seat and his bombsight was between his feet in its canvas case. The leader gunned his motors and taxied down the runway and Joe looked around into the darkened cabin. He could see the faces of the men, quiet and ready.

"Here we go," he said. He pushed the throttles a little forward and taxied behind the leader.

The thundering ships took off one behind the other. At 5,000 feet they made their formation. The men sat quietly at their stations, their eyes fixed. And the deep growl of the engines shook the air, shook the world, shook the future.